SCHOLASTIC

AF644748

ACTIVE English 6

Coursebook

Name: ______________________________

Class: ______________________________

Text credits:

Out of India: An Anglo-Indian Childhood by Jamila Gavin, first published by Pavilion Books Ltd, text copyright © Jamila Gavin 1997; *Chinese Cinderella* by Adeline Yen Mah, published by Penguin Group, Australia, 1999; Bharatan Kumarappa and the Navjivan Trust for *Aboard the Ship* from *The Story of My Life* (Scholastic India: 2006); *Catching Pheasants* by Manzu Islam, from *Tell Tales*, Volume 2, copyright © 2005 by flipped eye publishing limited. Reprinted by permission of flipped eye publishing limited; *Matilda* by Roald Dahl, first published by Jonathan Cape Ltd & Penguin Books Ltd; *Science Star Omar* from *Suffering Scientists* by Nick Arnold (Scholastic UK: 2000); *Focus on Disaster: Earthquake* by Fred Martin. Reprinted by permission of Capstone Global Library Ltd; *Rivers* by Catherine Chambers, first published by Heinemann Library, a division of Reed Educational and Professional Publishing Ltd, 2001; Anita Roy for *Trixy the Wonderdog* from *Superhero* (Scholastic India: 2007).

Photo credits:

Wikimedia
P8 © Steve Polyak; p9 © P. g. champion; p10 © Derek Voller; p11 © ILMOTOREDIRICERCA; p13 © Tevaprapas Makklay; p17 © crimfants, Omid RostamiNia, Hamachidori, Saleem Hameed; p19 © Mobiltel; p23 © TJArchi-Studio; p24 Source: The Jews in Tianjin, Government of Tianjin City, P.R.China; p34 © Lenny Francioni; p36 © Mtaylor848; p37 © gandhiserve.org, Dinodia; p47 © Bernard Gagnon; p48 © Tony Atkin; p55 © safetypinheart; p56 © Arpingstone, Dhirad, Simdaperce, DF08 at the English language Wikipedia, Shannon Hobbs, User:Hajor; p58 © Malene Thyssen; p59 © Bridges, Fidelia; p61 © Manfred Heyde; p62 © Rudolph. A. furtado; p64 © *Naumann, Naturgeschichte der Vögel Mitteleuropas*; p67 © Hans Hillewaert; p69 © Alisdair Mclean; p78 © Krzysztof Dreszer, Matthew Paul Argall; p80 © NASA/JPL; p83 © Adelaide Hanscom and Blanche Cumming; p91 © Ittiz at the English language Wikipedia, NASA/JPL/USGS; p94 © Ktrinko; p95 © Game McGimsey; p96 © Frank Domahs, Köln weitere Infos unter; p99 © Carolius Clusius, after van Neck; p103 © Webber Source; p105 © Midhun Kumar Allu; p106 © Luca Galuzzi; p107 © Denimedger; p110 © Jonathunder; p114 © mckaysavage; p118 © Haroldarmitage; p119 © Atunu; p121 © Rarelibra; p125 © M. Tawsif Salam; p128 © Ivan Zilic; p134 © David Castor; p144 © NASAs; p151 © snowyowls.

Every effort has been made to trace the copyright holders of material used in this book. If any copyright holder has been overlooked, we will make any necessary arrangements at the first opportunity.

First edition 2012
Reprinted 2012, 2014 (thrice), 2015 (twice), 2016 (Thrice), 2017 (Thrice), 2018, 2019, 2020, 2021, 2022, 2023, 2026

ISBN-978-81-8477-730-7

Printed in India at Saurabh Printers Pvt. Ltd.

Preface

The creators of SCHOLASTIC ACTIVE **English** believe that literacy acquisition is dependent on the integrated teaching of reading, writing, listening and speaking skills, and the engagement of students. This integrated approach to learning and literacy development is advocated through a systematic and consistent instructional design and scope and sequence.

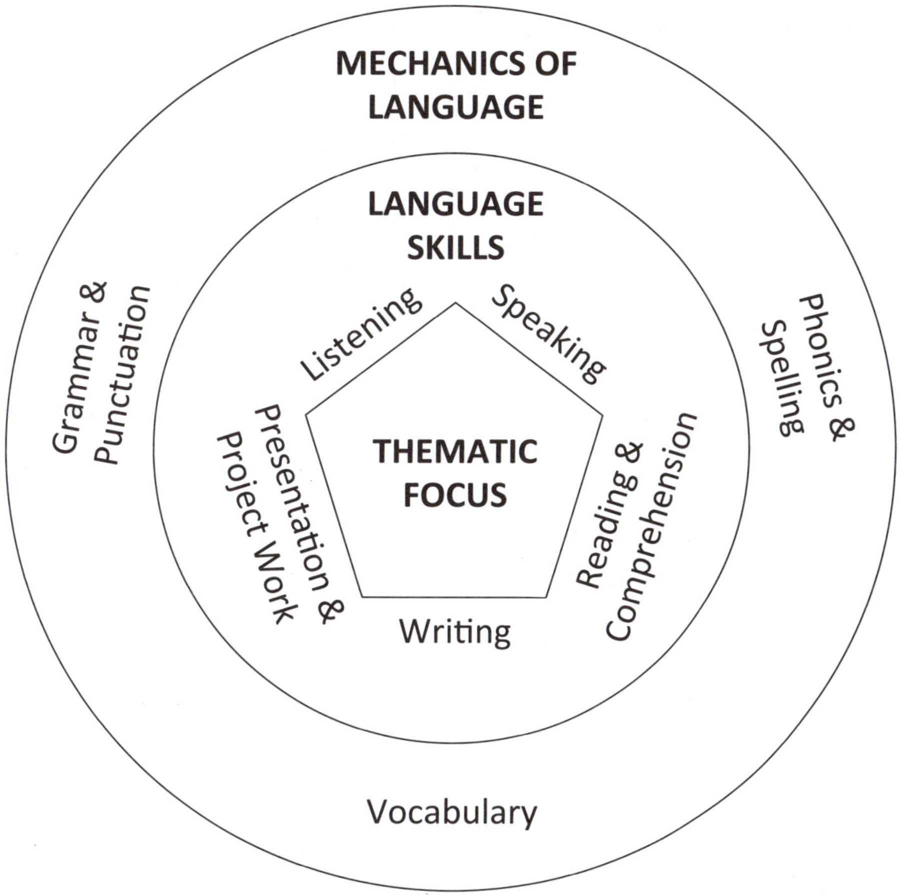

Each unit of the Coursebook has a thematic focus through which different language skills are meaningfully taught. Equal emphasis is given to each skill, enabling students to connect, transfer and build upon different skills.

Clear explanations and numerous examples give students a strong understanding of the mechanics of language and lay a strong foundation for good English.

As students progress through the levels, language skills are systematically taught at increasing levels of difficulty, allowing them to build upon small successes and reinforce the mechanics of language.

 ISBN-978-81-8477-730-7

Authentic and Varied Text Types

5 Pretty Words

Read the poem below by Elinor Wylie and answer the questions below.

1 Poets make pets of pretty, docile words:
I love smooth words, like gold-
enamelled fish
Which circle slowly with a silken swish,
And tender ones, like downy-feathered
birds:
Words shy and **dappled**, deep-eyed
deer in herds,
Come to my hand, and playful if I
wish,
Or purring softly at a silver dish,
Blue Persian kittens fed on cream
and curds.

2 I love bright words, words up and
singing early;
Words that are **luminous** in the dark,
and sing;

How does the poem change from one verse to the next?

enamelled: a layer of protective coating
dappled: spotted, speckled
luminous: glowing, shining

60 Theme 3: Self-expression

Authentic texts in a variety of text types engage students and prepare them for language in the real world.

Effective Instructional Design

G. Think of a synonym to replace the words in bold.

My **little** sister began secondary school last week, but she had no **inclination** to go at all. She thought the building was old and **ugly**, the playground too large and **uninviting** and the teachers and **students** very **unfriendly**. By the **end** of the first week we couldn't get her to come home. She loved it so much!

Grammar

A **coordinating conjunction** is a word that links the different thoughts, ideas and information within a sentence. It usually occurs in the middle of a sentence. Examples of coordinating conjunctions are **"and"**, **"but"**, **"so"**, **"or"** and **"yet"**.

Omar Khayyam was a scientist **and** a poet.

The coordinating conjunction "and" links two ideas together – Omar was a scientist and Omar was also a poet.

A. Join the sentence pairs with suitable coordinating conjunctions from the box below.

and	but	so	or	yet

1. Omar was born in Iran. We do not know anything about his family.
2. Omar Khayyam was interested in science. He became a teacher.
3. He did not find it easy to study. He became a great scholar.
4. He wrote a book about mathematics. He wrote another book about music.
5. Omar was busy teaching. He could not do as much research as he needed to.

88 Theme 4: The Natural World

A 'Show-Explain-Apply' methodology meets the needs of first generation English learners, making the lessons more achievable and boosting motivation.

Relevant and Meaningful Learning

12. Is there anything you particularly like about the poem *Pretty Words*? Write a few words about the poet's style.

Vocabulary

Alliteration is the repeated use of a particular letter or sound at the beginning of words or sets of words. It is a commonly used poetic device.

Take a second look at the verse in the previous section.

Sudden **s**wallows **s**wiftly **s**kimming,
Sunset's **s**lowly **s**preading **s**hade,
Silvery **s**ongsters **s**weetly **s**inging,
Summer's **s**oothing **s**erenade.

The "s" sound is repeated at the beginning of every word and hence the verse can be said to be "alliterative".

Sometimes, the recurring letters may appear in positions other than the beginning of words. For example:

The **rain** in **S**pain falls **main**ly on the **plain**s.

Alliteration is usually used to enhance the sound effect and rhythm of a poem. It also helps to emphasise an idea and support the theme. Apart from poems, alliteration is also used in advertising, leaflets, newspaper headlines and other non-fiction writing that aims to catch instant attention. Commercial organisations often use alliteration to make their brand names memorable. **C**oca-**C**ola, **D**unkin' **D**onuts, **A**merican **A**irlines are some examples.

Identify other examples of alliteration in the poem *Pretty Words*. Answer the following questions.

1. How many examples of alliteration can you find in the first stanza?
2. Choose two examples and say how they affect the overall impact of the poem.

Unit 5: Pretty Words 63

All language skills are meaningfully taught in the context of a theme, connecting the learning to real life and increasing learning enjoyment.

Active Learner Engagement

B. Imagine you are Adeline and that you are living in the French-style house described in the passage. Give a short description of some of the rooms in the house using the diagram below. Add branches to it if you like.

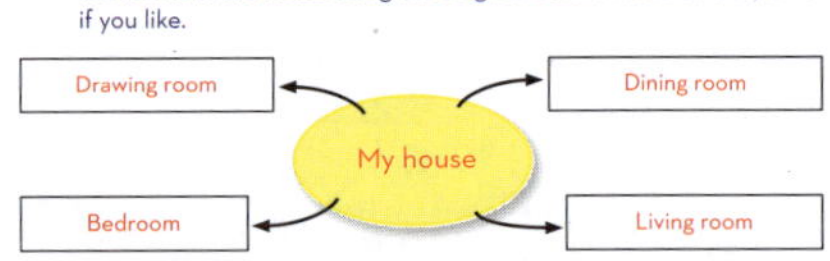

Activity

A **family tree** allows you to see at a glance the relationships between the members of a family.

Create Adeline's family tree using whatever information you can gather from the excerpt *Chinese Cinderella*. Follow the steps below.

1. Draw up a list of all the relatives Adeline lived with. Give names where you can. You can also use expressions such as "First Brother" or "Second Brother" in case the names are not available.
2. Create Adeline's family tree. Start with the oldest members of the family, as shown below. Include Adeline in the family tree as well.
3. The excerpt says Adeline's father married twice. Find a way to indicate it.

Adeline's family

Grandfather (Ye Ye) and Grandmother (Nai Nai)

Unit 2: Chinese Cinderella 33

Activities throughout the units encourage students to actively participate and learn, improving retention and increasing the interaction between teacher and students.

 ISBN-978-81-8477-730-7

Ongoing and Accurate Assessment

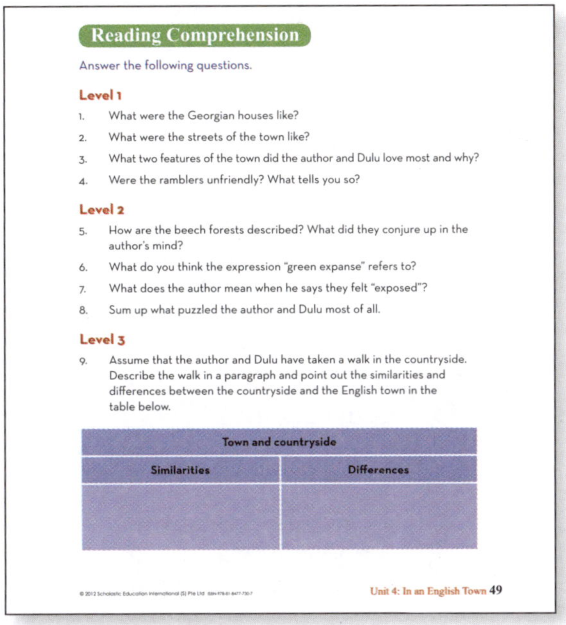

Reading Comprehension

Answer the following questions.

Level 1

1. What were the Georgian houses like?
2. What were the streets of the town like?
3. What two features of the town did the author and Dulu love most and why?
4. Were the ramblers unfriendly? What tells you so?

Level 2

5. How are the beech forests described? What did they conjure up in the author's mind?
6. What do you think the expression "green expanse" refers to?
7. What does the author mean when he says they felt "exposed"?
8. Sum up what puzzled the author and Dulu most of all.

Level 3

9. Assume that the author and Dulu have taken a walk in the countryside. Describe the walk in a paragraph and point out the similarities and differences between the countryside and the English town in the table below.

Town and countryside	
Similarities	Differences

Unit 4: In an English Town 49

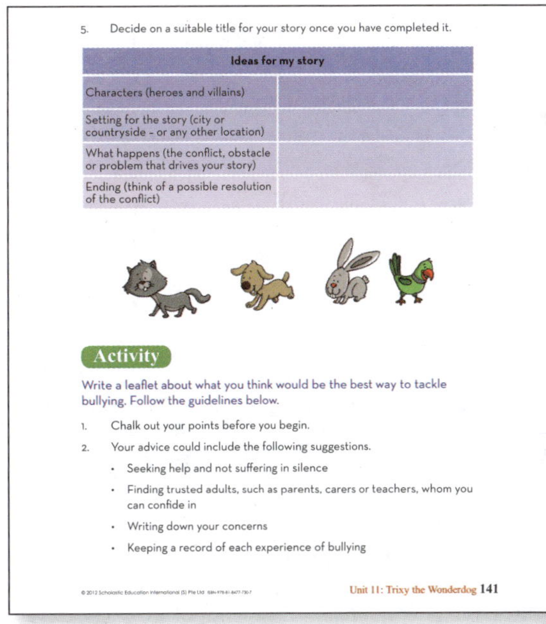

5. Decide on a suitable title for your story once you have completed it.

Ideas for my story	
Characters (heroes and villains)	
Setting for the story (city or countryside – or any other location)	
What happens (the conflict, obstacle or problem that drives your story)	
Ending (think of a possible resolution of the conflict)	

Activity

Write a leaflet about what you think would be the best way to tackle bullying. Follow the guidelines below.

1. Chalk out your points before you begin.
2. Your advice could include the following suggestions.
   - Seeking help and not suffering in silence
   - Finding trusted adults, such as parents, carers or teachers, whom you can confide in
   - Writing down your concerns
   - Keeping a record of each experience of bullying

Unit 11: Trixy the Wonderdog 141

Formative assessment throughout and summative assessment at the end of the units allow ongoing and accurate evaluation of students' understanding.

Diversity of Contexts

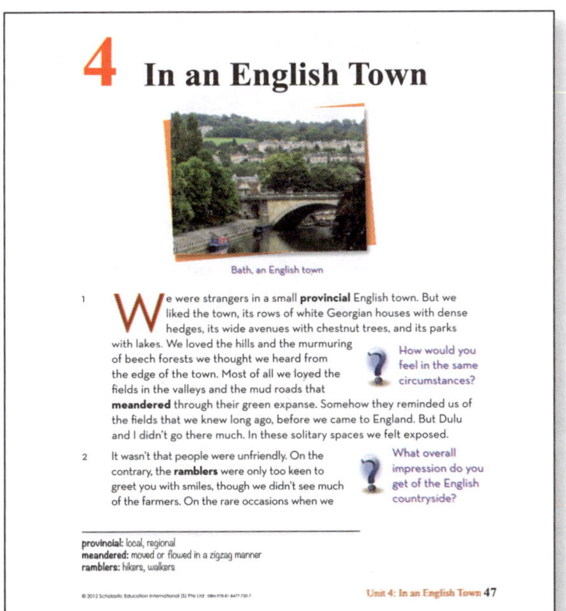

4 In an English Town

Bath, an English town

1 We were strangers in a small **provincial** English town. But we liked the town, its rows of white Georgian houses with dense hedges, its wide avenues with chestnut trees, and its parks with lakes. We loved the hills and the murmuring of beech forests we thought we heard from the edge of the town. Most of all we loved the fields in the valleys and the mud roads that **meandered** through their green expanse. Somehow they reminded us of the fields that we knew long ago, before we came to England. But Dulu and I didn't go there much. In these solitary spaces we felt exposed.

How would you feel in the same circumstances?

2 It wasn't that people were unfriendly. On the contrary, the **ramblers** were only too keen to greet you with smiles, though we didn't see much of the farmers. On the rare occasions when we

What overall impression do you get of the English countryside?

provincial: local, regional
meandered: moved or flowed in a zigzag manner
ramblers: hikers, walkers

Unit 4: In an English Town 47

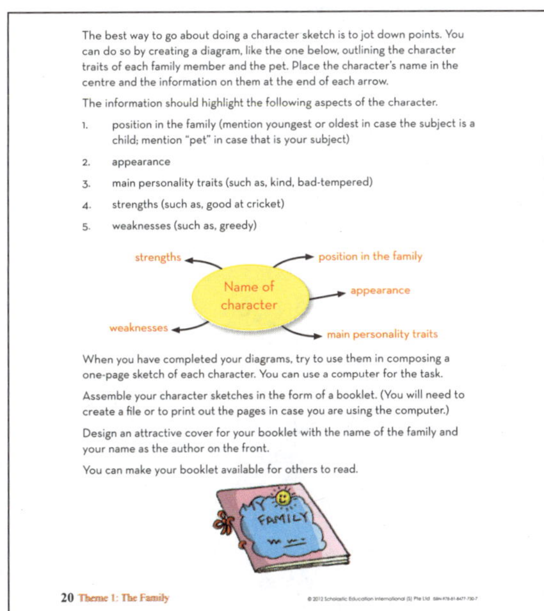

The best way to go about doing a character sketch is to jot down points. You can do so by creating a diagram, like the one below, outlining the character traits of each family member and the pet. Place the character's name in the centre and the information on them at the end of each arrow.

The information should highlight the following aspects of the character.

1. position in the family (mention youngest or oldest in case the subject is a child; mention "pet" in case that is your subject)
2. appearance
3. main personality traits (such as, kind, bad-tempered)
4. strengths (such as, good at cricket)
5. weaknesses (such as, greedy)

When you have completed your diagrams, try to use them in composing a one-page sketch of each character. You can use a computer for the task.

Assemble your character sketches in the form of a booklet. (You will need to create a file or to print out the pages in case you are using the computer.)

Design an attractive cover for your booklet with the name of the family and your name as the author on the front.

You can make your booklet available for others to read.

20 Theme 1: The Family

Familiar contexts provide relevance while international contexts broaden students' perspectives and prepare them to take the global stage.

We hope that all students will have fun in becoming active participants in their own learning and they will enjoy every success in the learning of English!

 ISBN-978-81-8477-730-7

Table of Contents

 ISBN-978-81-8477-730-7

Grammar/ Punctuation	Listening	Speaking	Writing	Activity
Common and Abstract nouns	Listen to passage on extended and nuclear family	Talk about your family	Create character sketches	Produce a timeline
Proper nouns	Listen to passage on Adeline Yen Mah	Talk about a character and a topic from *Chinese Cinderella*	Write diary entries	Create a family tree
Direct and indirect speech	Listen to passage on Gandhi	Act out a conversation	Write a conversation	Create a concept map
Prepositions/ prepositional phrases	Listen to passage on customs	Talk about a celebration	Write about two places, comparing one with the other	Skim the passage and collect information on a feast day
Rhyming words	Listen to another poem	Talk about poem by Lewis Carroll	Write a narrative with compound words	Create kennings and use them to compose poems
Linking and action verbs	Listen to another excerpt from *Matilda*	Talk about one or two characters from *Matilda*	Write a paragraph in the author's style	Write a blurb
Coordinating conjunctions	Listen to passage on the solar system	Talk about two planets, comparing one with the other	Write a biography	Create a fact file
Tenses in explanatory texts	Listen to passage on the Earth	Explain a natural phenomenon	Write about the Richter Scale	Collect information on earthquakes
Apostrophe to show contraction	Listen to passage on the Ganges	Talk about the Ganges	Create a leaflet	Complete a map
Active and passive voice	Listen to passage on Bangladesh	Talk about the cuisine of Bangladesh	Write a play	Create a fact file
Dash and ellipsis	Listen to excerpt from *Trixy the Wonderdog*	Narrate the story *Trixy the Wonderdog*	Write a story	Create a leaflet
Quantifying determiners	Listen to passage on dolphins	Talk about *Boy on a Dolphin*	Write an informative account	Create a poster

 ISBN-978-81-8477-730-7

Theme 1

The Family

A. Look at the picture.

1. Why do you think all these people are shown together?
2. What do you think they are doing?

B. Do you think it is important for a child to belong to a family?

1. Discuss the question with a partner and note down your reasons.
   Also write about the following.
   - All the things you do with your family
   - What you learn from your family
   - The occasions when you need your family the most
2. Review the notes you made and, between the two of you, identify what is the main reason the family is important for a child. Explain your point.
3. Discuss your main reason with other friends. Did they agree with you or did they have something else to say?

 ISBN-978-81-8477-730-7

1 Out of India

Read the following excerpt from *Out of India: An Anglo-Indian Childhood* by Jamila Gavin.

1 My first best friend was in England. I went to St Saviour's Primary School in Ealing, and there I met Doreen. Where I was dark-skinned with dark brown hair and eyes and obviously Indian, she was fair as day, with sparkling blue eyes and the most incredible head of tight, golden curls. We were completely inseparable.

Ealing Primary School

2 She lived with her mum, Aunty Blanche, and cousin Wendy over a shop in the Broadway. Aunty Blanche had skin as white as a ghost, and very black drawn-back hair and black penciled eyebrows. She was prone to fits. Wendy was a redhead with very freckled skin – and could truly be described as spiteful. Perhaps she was jealous of Doreen and me being such good friends. She was always trying to tag along and, as she was a bit older, seemed to delight in getting us to do things which could get us into trouble – like playing "chicken" across the railway line. Nor was she averse to a touch of blackmail which mostly amounted to: "I'll tell your mother on you."

How would you describe Aunty Blanche?

 ISBN-978-81-8477-730-7

3 On 4th September 1947, my mother gave birth to her fourth child, a girl. She wrote to us – Indra and I had been sent away to a farm at this time – and said she was calling the baby Rosemary. I was incredulous. Why Rosemary? She had never mentioned calling her by that name, and as far as I was concerned, it had no glamour whatsoever! "Why not Margaret?" I wrote back. The princesses Elizabeth and Margaret had the status of today's pop stars, though remembering all the famous stars of the time, I would probably have accepted Rita or Bette or Marlene. But Rosemary! It made no sense. So I refused to call her Rosemary, turning it neatly into Romie, which is what she has been called ever since.

4 My brother and I had been sent to a farm in the country for missionary children who needed care, while my mother had her baby. At first we were perfectly happy because it was St Julian's Farm, where we had been before, just outside Horsham which was then deepest country. It was where my belief in fairies was at its strongest; so strong that it almost hurt with the intensity. It's where I learned to sing the teasing song:

Terry, you're barmy

You went to join the army,

You got knocked out

With a bottle of stout,

Terry, you're barmy!

 ISBN-978-81-8477-730-7

5 We always had good times there and this was the end of August, so we joined in the harvesting from the hay carts pulled by huge **Shire horses**, blackberrying, making jam, exploring, playing in the streams. It was the England I adored. They had lots of books, and it was there I discovered Cicely Mary Barker's *Flower Fairies*, and through her caught many more glimpses of fairies than I would otherwise have done. I also learned to love and adore *Little Grey Rabbit*.

Did the author enjoy her stay at St Julian's farm? How do you know?

6 Then, tragedy. My mother wasn't ready to have us home, and we had to be moved on. We were taken by car along the coast to St Leonards-on-Sea. There was a large family house, in which lived a mother, father and daughter. I don't remember their names, except the daughter's name was Vivian. Sorry to all the really nice Vivians who have this very nice name, but I hated this girl so much that I've never been able to separate the name from her.

What was the author's impression of Vivian?

7 She was a tyrant – as were her parents. Because of them, my brother started wetting his bed; we were constantly punished...

Shire horses: large, strong workhorses used to pull heavy loads

 ISBN-978-81-8477-730-7

Reading Comprehension

A. Answer the following questions.

Level 1

1. Where did the author first meet Doreen? How does she describe her relationship with her?
2. How does the author compare her own appearance with Doreen's?
3. Where did Doreen live and with whom?
4. Briefly describe two of Doreen's family members.
5. Mention one good experience that the author has.
6. Mention one bad experience that the author has.
7. Where is the author sent while her mother is having a baby and who accompanies her?

Level 2

8. In paragraph 4, the author says that her "belief in fairies was at its strongest." Why do you think she says so?
9. How did the author and her brother spend their time in St Julian's farm? Did they enjoy themselves?
10. Name one of the books the author read during her stay at the farm.
11. What incident does the author describe as a "tragedy"? How do you think the author felt when the incident happened?
12. What are the various moods expressed by the author in the excerpt? You can use words from the box to frame your answer. Write down a few sentences explaining the reason behind each mood.

sad	lively	resigned	angry	resourceful
imaginative	disobedient	passionate	bad-tempered	

 ISBN-978-81-8477-730-7

Level 3

B. Read the second excerpt from *Out of India*, and answer the questions below.

1 It is cities that seem to make people cruel. Perhaps it is the breakdown of the community; the desperation that has driven so many people there, seeking to escape starvation or the poverty of village life if the delicate balance of **subsistence** breaks down. But the cruelty, particularly towards animals, which I saw in Indian cities such as Bombay, I didn't see in the countryside. There, where I saw working, animals like camels, buffaloes, elephants and horses they seemed to be valued and cared for by their owners.

2 Of all the animals in India, I loved the elephant the best. I still get a thrill out of seeing this huge beast walking with such casual, gentle, unaggressive elegance and the silence of its tread always astonishes me.

3 On the second anniversary of the Indian Independence we were all visiting relatives in a remote village. There was to be a procession of celebration down the village street, and we all turned out to watch.

---

subsistence: staying alive, survival

 ISBN-978-81-8477-730-7

13. How does Jamila Gavin feel about cities? Why does she feel that way? Do you agree with her?

14. The author has other opinions apart from the one she gives about cruelty in cities. She also mentions several facts. Find an opinion and a fact.

15. Complete the following opening sentences giving your own opinions about families in general.

    - I honestly think that ...
    - From my point of view ...
    - If you look at things from any mum's point of view ...
    - I have a lot of experience about ... and I can tell you that ...
    - If we're talking about families, I would say that ...

16. How were your childhood experiences? List some of your happy and sad experiences in the flow diagram below. You can add more branches to it if you want.

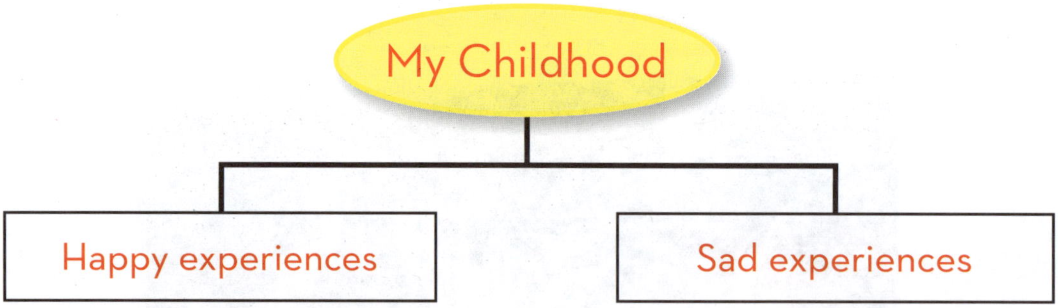

Vocabulary

A **simile** draws a comparison between two or more things using words such as **like** or **as**.

The **moon** was as bright **as** a **silver coin**.

 ISBN-978-81-8477-730-7

A. Can you find similes in the second passage?

(Note that when "like" or "as" is used, it does not always make a simile.) Underline the similes in the sentences below.

1. Her hands were as cold as ice.
2. The thief was as sly as a fox.
3. These biscuits taste like candies.
4. My brother stood beside me like a pillar of strength.
5. The tired traveller was sleeping like a log.

B. Create your own similes about the following.

1. an old shop that sells interesting things
2. railway lines
3. a fast-moving stream
4. a horse (or buffalo) pulling a cart
5. the experience of picking blackberries (or wild fruit) in the countryside

C. Record the ideas and your similes in a table like the one below. Mention them briefly, as in the example given in the chart.

Idea	Simile
old shop – full of antiques, interesting, (cluttered?)	

D. Make sentences with the following similes.

1. as blind as a bat
2. as alike as two peas in a pod

 ISBN-978-81-8477-730-7

3. as sweet as honey
4. like a giant among dwarfs
5. as different as night and day

Grammar

A **common noun** is a word we use in general to denote all members of a class of things, for example, **tree**, **dog**, **computer**.

An **abstract noun** is a word representing an idea or emotion, for example, **love**, **pride**.

A. Given below are some nouns taken from *Out of India: An Anglo-Indian Childhood*. Write them down in the following table under the correct headings.

belief trouble school blackmail child hair farm
glamour status baby jam sense house

Common nouns	Abstract nouns

 ISBN-978-81-8477-730-7

B. Now choose a common and an abstract noun from the list and combine them to form a single sentence like the one below. Write five such sentences of your own.

The **boy** laughed, despite the **trouble** he caused by spilling milk all over the table.

C. Write an abstract noun for each picture, which you think would best describe it.

a.

b.

c.

d.

 ISBN-978-81-8477-730-7

Listening

Listen to the passage and then answer the questions.

1. List the features of an extended family and a nuclear family in the table below.

Extended family	Nuclear family

2. What is the difference between an extended family and a nuclear family?
3. What is a kibbutz?
4. Give an example of a wild animal that prefers to stay with its extended family.

Speaking

What kind of a family do you live with, nuclear or extended? Do you think it is important to live in a family? Think carefully and answer the following questions.

1. Do you have brothers and sisters? Describe a favourite brother or sister. You can choose a cousin in case you don't have a sibling.
2. Do you have relatives living with you apart from your parents or guardians?
3. Do you have pets? If so, what are they like? Do you think pets are like family members?
4. What are the things you enjoy doing with your family? Describe a happy family moment.

 ISBN-978-81-8477-730-7

5. Describe any one of your grandparents. Is there anything you would like to do for them?

6. Form a group of three or four and each prepare a short talk about his or her family. Keep the following points in mind while making the presentation.
   - Describe the people you live with and what they are like.
   - Mention their appearance and their personality. Use similes where you can.
   - Don't forget to include your pets if you have any.
   - Finally, remember to be polite when you are talking about others.

Speaking Tips

- Speak clearly and naturally.
- Be confident.
- Do not look directly into the listeners' eyes, as doing so might cause distraction.
- If you make a mistake, correct yourself and carry on.

Writing

Write a character sketch of members of an imaginary family.

You may write about a grandmother, parent (mother or father) and two children, or an aunt, uncle and cousins, and so on. Make sure the family has at least three members.

Add a pet to your family. It could be any kind of pet – a cat, a dog or even an elephant!

 ISBN-978-81-8477-730-7

The best way to go about doing a character sketch is to jot down points. You can do so by creating a diagram, like the one below, outlining the character traits of each family member and the pet. Place the character's name in the centre and the information on them at the end of each arrow.

The information should highlight the following aspects of the character.

1. position in the family (mention youngest or oldest in case the subject is a child; mention "pet" in case that is your subject)
2. appearance
3. main personality traits (such as, kind, bad-tempered)
4. strengths (such as, good at cricket)
5. weaknesses (such as, greedy)

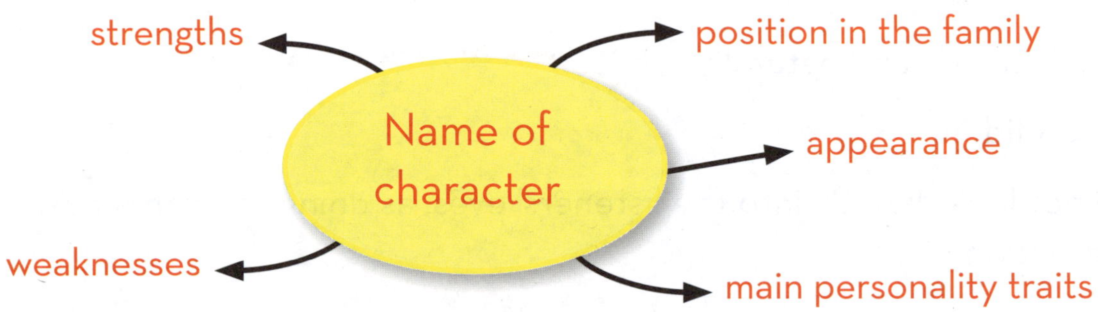

When you have completed your diagrams, try to use them in composing a one-page sketch of each character. You can use a computer for the task.

Assemble your character sketches in the form of a booklet. (You will need to create a file or to print out the pages in case you are using the computer.)

Design an attractive cover for your booklet with the name of the family and your name as the author on the front.

You can make your booklet available for others to read.

 ISBN-978-81-8477-730-7

Activity

In the first excerpt from *Out of India*, Jamila Gavin tells us what happened in England in chronological (time-specific) order. While some are happy memories, others are sad or troubled. However, they all affected her life as a child.

Read the excerpt again and mention what you think are the most important events in her life.

On the basis of your answer, create a timeline by following the steps below.

1. Make a copy of the timeline below and fill in the important events in order of sequence.
2. Add dates where you can.
3. Include your own comment regarding the effect it had on the author.

The timeline has been initiated for you.

Out of India (Excerpt 1)

Timeline of important events	Feelings
Meets Doreen at St Saviour's Primary School	*Happy, has a good friend*

 ISBN-978-81-8477-730-7

2 Chinese Cinderella

Read the following excerpt from *Chinese Cinderella* by Adeline Yen Mah.

1 At the time of my birth, Big Sister was six-and-a-half years old. My three brothers were five, four and three. They blamed me for causing Mama's death and never forgave me.

2 A year later, Father remarried. Our stepmother, whom we called Niang, was a seventeen-year-old Eurasian beauty fourteen years his junior. Father always introduced her to his friends as his "French wife" though she was actually half French and half Chinese. Besides Chinese, she spoke French and English. She was almost as tall as Father, stood very straight and dressed only in French clothes – many of which came from Paris. Her thick, wavy, black hair never had a curl out of place. Her large, dark-brown eyes were fringed with long, thick lashes. She wore heavy make-up, expensive French perfume and many diamonds and pearls. It was Grandmother Nai Nai who told us to call her Niang, another Chinese term for "mother".

What do you think the term "Eurasian beauty" means?

3 A year after their wedding, they had a son (Fourth Brother) followed by a daughter (Little Sister). There were now seven of us: five children from Father's first wife and two from our stepmother, Niang.

4 Apart from Father and Niang, we lived with Grandfather Ye Ye, Grandmother Nai Nai and Aunt Baba in a big house in the French Concession of Tianjin, a city port on the north-east coast of China. Aunt Baba was our father's older sister. As she was meek, shy, unmarried and had no money of her own, my parents ordered her to take care of me. From an early age, I slept in a cot in her room. This suited me well because that way I grew to

Who all were the members of the family?

 ISBN-978-81-8477-730-7

know her better and better. Perhaps inevitably, under the circumstances, we came to love each other very deeply and to share a life apart from the rest of the family.

5 Many years ago, China had lost a war (known as the Opium War) against England and France. As a result, many coastal cities in China (such as Tianjin and Shanghai) came to be occupied by foreign soldiers.

What was the French-style house like?

6 The conquerors parcelled out the best areas of these treaty ports for themselves, claiming them as their "territories" or "concessions". Tianjin's French Concession was like a little piece of Paris transplanted into the centre of this big Chinese city. Our house was built in the French style and looked as if it had been lifted from one of the tree-shaded avenues near the Eiffel Tower. Surrounded by a charming garden, it had porches, balconies, bow windows, awnings and a slanted tile roof. Across the street stood St Louis Catholic Boy's School, where the teachers were French missionaries.

French-style building

 ISBN-978-81-8477-730-7

7 In December 1941, when the Japanese bombed Pearl Harbor, the United States became involved in the Second World War. Although Tianjin was occupied by the Japanese, the French Concession continued to be governed by French officials. French policemen strutted about looking important and barking out orders in their own language, which they expected everyone to understand and obey.

What were the French policemen like?

Tianjin as it was in the 1940s

Tianjin as it is today

Reading Comprehension

A. Answer the following questions.

Level 1

1. Who did Adeline's father remarry and how old was she?
2. What did Niang look like? Describe in brief.
3. How many children did Adeline's father have a year after he married Niang?
4. Who was Adeline close to? Why?
5. Why were foreign soldiers stationed in large numbers in many of China's coastal cities?

 ISBN-978-81-8477-730-7

6. What did the author's house in Tianjin look like?
7. What major world event took place in December 1941?
8. What effect did the event have on Tianjin?

Level 2

9. Do you think the opening paragraph is powerful? Explain.
10. What effect did Adeline's mother's death have on Adeline's family?
11. Why do you think Adeline's family house was built in the French style? What were its chief attractions?
12. How does the author describe the French policemen?
13. What do you think she feels about them?

B. Read the excerpt once more and answer the following questions.

Level 3

Since *Chinese Cinderella* is an autobiography, the story is told in chronological order. Many of the paragraphs begin by using **time connectors** to show the order of events. For example, the first paragraph opens with the time connector "**At the time**".

14. Can you find more time connectors in the subsequent paragraphs?
    - Complete the table on the next page, listing separately the time connectors used at the beginning of the paragraphs and those within the paragraphs. Remember you are only looking for connectors related to time (or sequence).

 ISBN-978-81-8477-730-7

Time connectors	
At the beginning of paragraphs	**Within paragraphs**
At the time	

- Looking at the table, can you identify the connectors which take us back to the time before Adeline was born and those which take us forward into her life? List them separately.

15. Can you think of other kinds of time connectors that may help us sequence ideas? Try and add at least eight more to the above list. For example, before, during.

16. Briefly describe an interesting experience you had, using time connectors.

Vocabulary

Adjectives are describing words. They are used to describe people, animals, places and things. Adjectives add details to a story and make it more interesting.

A. A number of adjectives are used to describe the character Niang in the excerpt from *Chinese Cinderella*. Can you identify them? Write them down next to the nouns they qualify in the table.

 ISBN-978-81-8477-730-7

Nouns	Adjectives
hair	
eyes	
eyelashes	
make-up	
perfume	

B. What impression do you get of Aunt Baba? Find the adjectives that describe her in paragraph 4 and list them down. You can also use them to label the illustration.

Aunt Baba

 ISBN-978-81-8477-730-7

C. What other adjectives can you think of to describe Aunt Baba? Add a few of them to your list in question B.

D. Write a brief description of Aunt Baba using some of the adjectives in your list. Focus on the following aspects.

1. Her position in the family
2. Adeline's parents' attitude towards her
3. Her relationship with Adeline

E. Read the adjectives listed below. They are synonyms of some of the adjectives used in the excerpt from *Chinese Cinderella*. Match them with the corresponding adjectives in the excerpt. Use the paragraph numbers to help you.

Synonym	Adjective in the excerpt
upright	paragraph 2:
enormous	paragraph 4:
elder	paragraph 4:
finest	paragraph 6:
paths	paragraph 6:
attractive	paragraph 6:
sloping	paragraph 6:

 ISBN-978-81-8477-730-7

F. Some adjectives lose their meaning and impact due to overuse. Find synonyms for these commonly used adjectives and write them down.

1. nice
2. good
3. bad
4. funny
5. really

G. Write down four adjectives to describe each of the following nouns.

1. sunrise
2. a frog
3. a diver
4. a maharaja
5. a pineapple

H. Write a sentence for each of these pairs of adjectives. One example is done for you.

> enormous / pink
>
> An enormous pink balloon flew past the window.

1. white / fluffy
2. tiny / scampering
3. fresh / colourful
4. lovely / happy
5. relieved / hopeful

 ISBN-978-81-8477-730-7

Grammar

A **proper noun** is the name of a person, a place or a specific thing (such as the months of the year or the days of the week).

A. Several proper nouns have been written incorrectly in the following paragraphs. Read first, and make corrections.

Adeline yen mah was sent away to st joseph's college, a boarding school, where she spent three years virtually cut off from her family and her beloved aunt baba. Little did she know that all the letters she wrote to aunt baba were never received. In fact, the letters landed up in the hands of her stepmother, niang, instead of aunt baba.

Adeline was fourteen, and her time at st joseph's was drawing to a close. All who knew her believed she would be unable to pursue higher education and that she would now have to find work for herself. However, she won a writing competition while still at st joseph's, and her father relented as adeline's success reflected well on him and his family. So adeline was allowed to study medicine in the united kingdom. She attended the london hospital medical school.

B. Correct the mistakes in these sentences.

1. mr and mrs patel decided that they would visit their daughter who was at the school of music and dance in a nearby city.
2. Last week I went with my mother to see the taj mahal in agra because I had never visited it before.
3. dr desai was having the surgery painted by the local painter mr chopra and his son dinesh.
4. I love to go to the movies with my grandmother and yesterday we went to kolkata to see *chak de! india* again.

 ISBN-978-81-8477-730-7

5. The famous american actress marilyn monroe's real name was norma jean.
6. Did you know that the famous west indian cricketer sir vivian richards was also awarded the obe for his service to cricket?

C. Write down the answer to the ten questions correctly. (Be careful! One of them is a trick question.)

1. Name your favourite book.
2. Name your favourite film.
3. Name your favourite film actor.
4. Name your favourite pop star.
5. Name your favourite animal.
6. Name the first and ninth month of the year.
7. Name any three cities in India.
8. Name three countries in Asia.
9. Name the capital of England and its famous clock.
10. Name the other countries in the UK and their capitals.

Listening

Listen to the passage and then answer the questions.

1. Would you consider Adeline a strong woman despite the fact that she never received a mother's love? If so, where do you think she drew strength from?
2. Describe Adeline's grand-aunt who was born in the nineteenth century and was well known in her time.

 ISBN-978-81-8477-730-7

Speaking

A. Work in pairs. Describe Aunt Baba to your partner. Dwell on the following in your talk.

1. Your impression of Aunt Baba
2. How she influenced Adeline

B. What do you know about the Opium War? Work with your partner and collect information on this historical event. Organise the information and present a short talk to the class on the topic. Make sure your presentation includes the following points.

1. Cause of the event
2. Duration of the event (including starting and ending dates)
3. Consequences of the event

Writing

A. Choose three events from *Chinese Cinderella*, which you believe affected Adeline, and write diary entries. (For example, one entry could be about her father marrying Niang.) Follow the guidelines below.

1. Use fictional dates for your diary entries, but bear in mind that Adeline was born in 1937.
2. Make sure you use the first person "I" since you are writing from Adeline's point of view.

 ISBN-978-81-8477-730-7

B. Imagine you are Adeline and that you are living in the French-style house described in the passage. Give a short description of some of the rooms in the house using the diagram below. Add branches to it if you like.

Activity

A **family tree** allows you to see at a glance the relationships between the members of a family.

Create Adeline's family tree using whatever information you can gather from the excerpt *Chinese Cinderella*. Follow the steps below.

1. Draw up a list of all the relatives Adeline lived with. Give names where you can. You can also use expressions such as "First Brother" or "Second Brother" in case the names are not available.
2. Create Adeline's family tree. Start with the oldest members of the family, as shown below. Include Adeline in the family tree as well.
3. The excerpt says Adeline's father married twice. Find a way to indicate it.

Adeline's family

Grandfather (Ye Ye) and Grandmother (Nai Nai)

 ISBN-978-81-8477-730-7

Theme 2

Time and Place

A. Look at the photograph above.

1. Where do you think it was taken?
2. What are these people doing?
3. Can you guess how they are feeling?

B. Have you ever lived or travelled abroad? If so, what was the experience like? Did anything feel strange? In case you never went abroad, try and imagine what it would feel like to do so.

1. Share your thoughts with a partner. Make notes about the following.
   - The language you would speak
   - The habits and customs
   - The things you liked best
   - The things you missed
2. Review your notes and decide whether for you the overwhelming feeling would be one of homesickness or of excitement at experiencing new things.

 ISBN-978-81-8477-730-7

3 Aboard the Ship

Read the following passage. Mohandas Karamchand Gandhi, commonly known as Mahatma Gandhi (1869–1948), is one of India's most famous historical figures. As a young man, he travelled to both England and South Africa. This excerpt is taken from his autobiography *The Story of My Life*, which describes his journey to England.

1 I was not used to talking in English, and except for Shri Mazmudar all the other passengers in the second saloon were English. I could not speak to them. I could rarely follow their remarks when they came up to speak to me, and even when I understood I could not reply. I had to frame every sentence in my mind before I could bring it out. I was innocent of the use of knives and forks and had not the boldness to inquire what dishes on the menu were free of meat. I, therefore, never took meals at the table but always had them in my cabin, and they consisted principally of sweets and fruits, which I had brought with me. Shri Mazmudar had no difficulty, and he mixed with everybody. He would move about freely on the deck, while I hid myself in the cabin the whole day, only going up on the deck when there were but few people. Shri Mazmudar kept pleading with me to associate with the passengers and to talk with them freely. He advised me to take every possible opportunity of talking in English and not mind making mistakes, which were obviously unavoidable with a foreign tongue. But nothing could make me conquer my shyness.

What impression do you form of Gandhi in this paragraph?

How does Shri Mazmudar's personality contrast with Gandhi's?

 ISBN-978-81-8477-730-7

What impression does the English passenger make on Gandhi?

2 An English passenger, wanting to be nice to me, drew me into conversation. He was older than I. He asked me what I ate, where I was going, why I was shy, and so on. He also advised me to come to the table. He laughed at my insistence on not eating meat, and said in a friendly way while we were crossing the Red Sea, "It is all very well so far, but you will have to change your decision in the Bay of Biscay. And it is so cold in England that one cannot possibly live there without meat."

3 "But I have heard that people can live there without eating meat," I said.

4 "Rest assured it is a lie," said he. "No one, to my knowledge, lives there without being a meat-eater. Don't you see that I am not asking you to take liquor, though I do so? But I do think you should eat meat, for you cannot live without it."

5 "I thank you for your kind advice, but I have solemnly promised my mother not to touch meat. If it be found impossible to get on without it, I will far rather go back to India."

6 We entered the Bay of Biscay, but I did not begin to feel the need either of meat or of liquor. We reached Southampton, as far as I remember, on a Saturday.

7 Someone on board had advised us to put up at the Victoria Hotel in London. Shri Mazmudar and I found the hotel to be a trying affair. It was also very expensive. There was, however, a Sindhi fellow passenger from Malta who had become friends with Shri Mazmudar, and as he was not a stranger to London, he offered to find rooms for us. We agreed, and on Monday, as soon as we got our baggage, we paid our bills and went to the rooms rented for us by the Sindhi friend. I remember my hotel bill came to £3, an amount which shocked me. And I had

 ISBN-978-81-8477-730-7

practically starved in spite of this heavy bill! For I could relish nothing. When I did not like one thing, I asked for another, but I had to pay for both just the same. The fact is that all this while I had depended on the foodstuffs which I had brought with me from Bombay.

8 I was very uneasy even in the new rooms. I would continually think of my home and country, and of my mother's love. At night the tears would stream down my cheeks, and home memories of all sorts made sleep out of the question. It was impossible to share my misery with anyone. And even if I could have done so, where was the use? I knew of nothing that would soothe me. Everything was strange – the people, their ways, and even their dwellings. I was a complete stranger to English etiquette and continually had to be on my guard. There was the additional inconvenience of the vegetarian vow. Even the dishes that I could eat were tasteless. I thus found myself between **Scylla and Charybdis**. England I could not bear, but to return to India was not to be thought of. Now that I had come, I must finish the three years, said the inner voice.

Gandhi in his youth

Gandhi in his later years

Scylla and Charybdis: two sea monsters from Greek mythology, who were believed to haunt the Strait of Messina between Italy and Sicily and terrorise sailors. Scylla frequented the shores of Italy and Charybdis those of Sicily.

 ISBN-978-81-8477-730-7

Reading Comprehension

Answer the following questions.

Level 1

1. Where was Gandhi travelling to?
2. Why did Gandhi prefer to have his meals in his cabin rather than at the table with his co-passengers? How different were Shri Mazmudar's eating habits?
3. What advice did the English passenger give to Gandhi and what was the latter's response?
4. How much was the bill at the hotel? How did Gandhi react to it?
5. What food did Gandhi primarily depend on during his stay at the hotel?
6. Why did Gandhi feel uneasy in the new rooms?
7. What was the "additional inconvenience" and how did it affect his stay in London?
8. What did Gandhi's inner voice say to him?

Level 2

9. How old do you think Gandhi was when he sailed to England? Mention the clues that have helped you answer.
10. How would you describe Gandhi's mood on board the ship?
11. Why do you think Gandhi went to London? What clues did you find in the excerpt?
12. What are the things Gandhi missed about his motherland? What aspect of his personality is expressed through his thoughts and feelings?
13. What does "inner voice" refer to? Why do you think Gandhi listened to it?

 ISBN-978-81-8477-730-7

Level 3

14. What does the saying "between Scylla and Charybdis" mean in the passage? Can you say which of the following means more or less the same?

    - No good crying over spilt milk
    - Better safe than sorry
    - Between the devil and the deep blue sea
    - It's an ill wind that blows nobody any good
    - Never fish in troubled waters
    - All that glitters is not gold

15. Do you know what the sayings in the bulleted list mean? If not, try to find out. Take turns with your partner to explain them one by one.

Vocabulary

In a dictionary, most words and phrases have more than one meaning. However, when we read them in sentences, we interpret them according to the way they are used. The text that surrounds a particular word or expression determines its **contextual meaning**.

A. Read the following table below. All the words and expressions can be found in the excerpt *Aboard the Ship*. Do you know what they mean?

1. Find the words and expressions in the excerpt above. What do they mean?

 ISBN-978-81-8477-730-7

2. Write down another word or expression for each one under the column "Similar words or expressions". Note that their meaning must be the same as in the excerpt.

Words and expressions	Similar words or expressions
conquer	
rest assured	
liquor	
a trying affair	
relish nothing	
dwellings	
English etiquette	
vow	
the inner voice	

3. Add at least three more words and expressions from the passage in the left-hand column of the table. Write down similar expressions or synonyms in the space provided.

B. Match these expressions to their meanings.

1. a dog's breakfast — like father or mother
2. under a cloud — no money

 ISBN-978-81-8477-730-7

3.	carried away	in trouble
4.	at a loose end	overexcited
5.	hard up	a mess
6.	a chip of the old block	nothing to do

C. Think of expressions that have these words in them and write them down. You can carry out research if you need to, with your teacher's guidance. Discuss what the expressions mean with your partner. One example is done for you.

easy

Easy does it. Go easy on him/her.

1. heart
2. day
3. apple
4. weather
5. cat

D. Write a conversation (as a script) between two friends about their day at school. Include these expressions in the conversation.

1. I'm all ears
2. wasn't up to the mark
3. in the same boat

 ISBN-978-81-8477-730-7

Grammar

When the words spoken by a character or person are written verbatim, it is termed **direct speech**. We use speech marks to distinguish such words from the rest of the text.

speech marks only enclose the exact words spoken

"But I have heard that people can live there without eating meat," I said.

Indirect or **reported speech** is not enclosed within speech marks because it only reproduces the meaning of what has been said and may not use the actual words of the speaker. Also, indirect speech does not have the same impact as that of direct speech, so it might use additional words to indicate the feeling or mood of the speaker.

tells us how the speaker is feeling

the word "that" is often used in indirect speech

He **declared that** I should rest assured it was a lie and that no one, to **his** knowledge, lived there without being a meat eater.

the first person personal pronoun "my" changes to third person "his"

A. Convert the following direct speech into indirect speech. Make sure you mention who is speaking and, if necessary, indicate the feeling or mood underlying the words.

1. "But I have heard that people can live there without eating meat," I said.
2. "I thank you for your kind advice, but I have solemnly promised my mother not to touch meat."

 ISBN-978-81-8477-730-7

B. Now turn the following sentence taken from the excerpt into direct speech.

Shri Mazmudar kept pleading with me to associate with the passengers and to talk with them freely.

C. Add speech marks and other punctuation in the correct places.

Whack shouted Jem as he hit the ball with a resounding thud.

Jason tried to catch it but the ball went zooming across the playing field.

Oh no he shouted, but before he could give chase Tom was after it.

When he reached the boundary fence Tom couldn't see the ball anywhere.

Then suddenly he called out got it and came running back to the others.

D. Change the following into direct speech. You can leave out or add some words, but be careful not to change the meaning.

Irma showed her mum the new dress she had bought at Zena's shop, but when she tried it on it was much too tight. Mum said she shouldn't worry and that she should take the dress back the next day and see if she could get a bigger size.

E. Change the following into indirect speech. Again, you can leave out or add some words, but the meaning must be the same.

"Well done, Deepak," said the teacher as he passed the homework book to him. "I'm glad to see you've done it all extremely well this week," he added, frowning at Freda, who had left her book at home. "If your brother can manage to get it done, so can you!"

 ISBN-978-81-8477-730-7

Listening

Listen to the passage. The events mentioned occurred in two different places – India and London. Fill in the table to show the main events that took place at each of these places.

India	London

Speaking

Team up with a partner and act out the conversation below. Follow the guidelines.

1. Read the conversation and choose a role each.
2. Learn your part by heart and perform your respective roles. Make sure you use the exact words in the dialogue.
3. Carry on with the conversation for three more minutes by improvising more dialogue (making up your own words).

The stranger faced Jack and asked, "Can you tell me the way to the Waterloo underground station, please?"

Jack pointed to a restaurant and replied, "You're nearly there. You'll find the underground station once you cross the first turning on the right, past that restaurant."

 ISBN-978-81-8477-730-7

Writing

Read paragraphs 2 to 5 of the excerpt *Aboard the Ship* and write a probable sequel to the conversation between Gandhi and the English passenger. Your composition should cover at least a page. You may keep the following points in mind.

1. Gandhi's determination to avoid meat and the English passenger's argument that it would be impossible to survive on a vegetarian diet in England during that season as it would be too cold.
2. The pronoun "I" is used to record direct speech.

Activity

Imagine you are making a trip to another country for further studies. Work in pairs to find out all about the country you are going to. Follow the guidelines below.

1. Choose the country you would like to visit. Ask your partner to do the same.

 ISBN-978-81-8477-730-7

2. Create a concept map indicating all the aspects of the country you feel you should be aware of. For example:

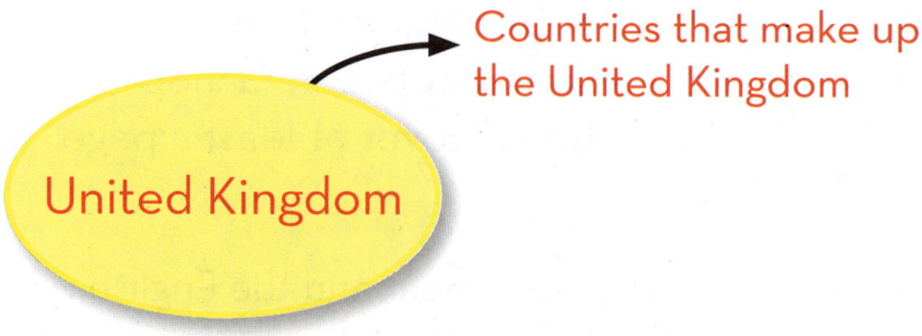

3. Create as many branches as you would need to cover all the essential topics such as customs, currency and languages spoken.
4. Choose a city where you would like to stay for your studies and make a separate concept map on it. You will need to do substantial research for both the maps. Ask your teacher for guidance if you use the Internet.
5. Compare your concept map with that of your partner. What can you learn from each other?

 ISBN-978-81-8477-730-7

4 In an English Town

Bath, an English town

1 We were strangers in a small **provincial** English town. But we liked the town, its rows of white Georgian houses with dense hedges, its wide avenues with chestnut trees, and its parks with lakes. We loved the hills and the murmuring of beech forests we thought we heard from the edge of the town. Most of all we loved the fields in the valleys and the mud roads that **meandered** through their green expanse. Somehow they reminded us of the fields that we knew long ago, before we came to England. But Dulu and I didn't go there much. In these solitary spaces we felt exposed.

How would you feel in the same circumstances?

2 It wasn't that people were unfriendly. On the contrary, the **ramblers** were only too keen to greet you with smiles, though we didn't see much of the farmers. On the rare occasions when we

What overall impression do you get of the English countryside?

---

provincial: local, regional
meandered: moved or flowed in a zigzag manner
ramblers: hikers, walkers

 ISBN-978-81-8477-730-7

ventured beyond the town, we would wonder about the well-cultivated fields. No one would be tilling the land or reaping the harvests. We would look at each other and wonder by what miracle these fields became so abundant with crops. Everywhere you looked you saw evidence of human hands at work: the well-ordered fences, the ditches, and the planned wilderness of bushes. Yet we hardly ever saw anyone working on them.

A. Skim through "In an English Town", an excerpt from *Catching Pheasants* by Manzu Islam, and see if you can figure out the overall subject matter. Try using the following skimming methods one by one: reading every few words, reading down the middle and reading key sentences.

B. Did you use any other method to skim? Write down how you skimmed or choose from the following.

1. Checked the topic sentences in each paragraph.
2. Skipped words, reading from left to right.
3. Ran eyes down the middle of the text.

C. Try skimming again using the methods you did not use the first time. Which method seems to give the most accurate information?

D. Now you may read the excerpt line by line.

 ISBN-978-81-8477-730-7

Reading Comprehension

Answer the following questions.

Level 1

1. What were the Georgian houses like?
2. What were the streets of the town like?
3. What two features of the town did the author and Dulu love most and why?
4. Were the ramblers unfriendly? What tells you so?

Level 2

5. How are the beech forests described? What did they conjure up in the author's mind?
6. What do you think the expression "green expanse" refers to?
7. What does the author mean when he says they felt "exposed"?
8. Sum up what puzzled the author and Dulu most of all.

Level 3

9. Assume that the author and Dulu have taken a walk in the countryside. Describe the walk in a paragraph and point out the similarities and differences between the countryside and the English town in the table below.

Town and countryside	
Similarities	**Differences**

 ISBN-978-81-8477-730-7

Vocabulary

In the excerpt *In an English Town*, the author says in the last line, "Yet we hardly ever saw anyone working on them (the fields)." The word "hardly" qualifies the verb "saw" as it tells us at what pace the event alluded to occurred. It is an example of what is termed **adverb of frequency**.

adverb of frequency → **hardly**; verb → **saw**

"Yet we **hardly** ever **saw** anyone working on them."

A. Can you find another word or expression in the paragraph that means the same as "hardly"?

Adverbs of frequency can be positioned differently in a sentence according to what is being conveyed. Look at sentences A and B below.

A: I **often** go to the cinema.

B: I go to the cinema, **often**.

In sentence B, the word "often" is placed at the end so that it comes across as an afterthought. In sentence A, the same word asserts the time factor clearly at the outset. This is the more common usage.

B. Look at the sentences below. Place each adverb, given in brackets, where you think it rightly belongs in the sentence. Note that there may be more than one place in a sentence where a given adverb may appear suitable. The following is an example.

The author went walking in the fields. (seldom)
The author **seldom** went walking in the fields.

1. They kept to the town, and did not explore the countryside much. (usually)
2. The houses in the town were Georgian in style. (often)

 ISBN-978-81-8477-730-7

3. The ramblers hiked along the country paths. (regularly)

4. You could hear the beech trees swaying in the wind. (sometimes)

C. Write down in the table below three adverbs of frequency that mean the same as those in the left-hand column. Think of adverbs that have not been used already.

Adverbs	**Synonyms**
always	
sometimes	
never	

D. Choose a suitable adverb of frequency from the list and add them to the sentences below in a suitable place.

now and then | twice | ever | monthly | annually

1. Is he going to pack his school bag properly?
2. The class takes place at the new college in the South Wing.
3. The goats chewed everything, so she certainly won't forget to shut the gate.
4. The celebrations occur when the pavilion is available and the cost of hiring it is not too high.
5. You can see the stork wading in the shallows if you are patient and make no noise.

E. In each of the sentences underline the adverb of frequency and the verb it relates to.

1. Grace and her family rarely visit her grandparents because they live too far away.

 ISBN-978-81-8477-730-7

2. Occasionally Jamila collects her small brother from school and takes him to the park.

3. The festival generally begins with singing and dancing and a band playing by the lake.

4. Every day that greedy cat asks for food from the neighbours even though she's well fed by her owners.

5. We often meet up with our friends to have a picnic and a bike ride or a game of cricket.

F. Write sentences using these adverbs of frequency.

1. every half-hour
2. daily
3. weekly
4. every fortnight

Grammar

We use **prepositions** to indicate the relationship between two or more nouns in a sentence.

The **bird** (noun) sang **in** (preposition) the **tree** (noun).

The phrase "in the tree" is an example of what is termed **prepositional phrase**. A prepositional phrase begins with a preposition.

The bird sang **in the tree**. (prepositional phrase)

 ISBN-978-81-8477-730-7

A. Look at paragraph 1 of the excerpt *In an English Town*. Make a list of all the prepositional phrases that begin with the preposition "with".

B. Underline the prepositions and circle the prepositional phrases in the following sentences.

1. The cows are grazing in the meadow by the stream.
2. The Sun's rays shone on the water.
3. The rabbit ran across the field and into the wood.
4. Wild flowers grew along the path.
5. They came up to the house beside the river.

C. Write your own sentences with the following prepositions.

1. beyond
2. through
3. beneath
4. within
5. over

D. Circle the prepositions in this list.

box cloud during about street from station form

E. Complete the sentences with suitable prepositions.

1. The car trailed ______________ the lorry and the van.
2. The monsoon rains ______________ Mumbai are over.
3. The horse took a mighty leap ______________ the high fence.
4. Jasper bought a skateboard ______________ red wheels.

 ISBN-978-81-8477-730-7

F. Use these nouns and prepositional phrases in sentences.

1. baseball hat / next to the lamp
2. mask / with gold patterns
3. bird / on top of the roof
4. panel / behind the bookshelf
5. jar / above the fridge

Listening

Listen to the passage and complete the table.

1. Compare and contrast the practices in the past and today by completing the column "In the past" in the table below.

In the past	Today
	• Coloured eggs and chocolate eggs are sold in shops.
	• The chocolate rabbit is a common sight.
	• Decorated bonnets are seldom seen now.

 ISBN-978-81-8477-730-7

2. What celebration is mentioned in the passage?

Speaking

Make a group of three or four and find out six more things about the celebration discussed in "Listening".

1. Consider the religious significance of this celebration and the popular culture behind it.
2. Decide what each member will speak on. Take turns to present your talk.

 ISBN-978-81-8477-730-7

Writing

A. Study each photograph carefully. In which country do you think each was clicked?

1. 

2. 

3. 

4. 

5. 

6. 

 ISBN-978-81-8477-730-7

B. Each photograph contains clues about the place where it was taken. List down the clues contained in each photograph separately and verify your answers once you finish.

C. Choose two photographs and note down their similarities and differences in the table below. Choose an appropriate title for the table, referring to the names of the places.

Title:	
Similarities	**Differences**

D. Study the table and compose a paragraph each on the similarities and differences between the two places.

Activity

A. Briefly skim through the passage below focusing on the key sentences. Note that key sentences are not necessarily those that open paragraphs.

B. Gather information on a feast day in any cultural celebration and use it to write a paragraph.

 ISBN-978-81-8477-730-7

C. Ask a partner to skim through your paragraph and to write a summary of it.

1 Many festivals across the world were initiated by early farming communities and usually have something to do with the seasons. The rainy season, for instance, is a joyous time for most agricultural people as it promises bumper crops. Likewise, spring is associated with birth and new beginnings. Seasons such as these call for celebration and festivity as they hold the promise of happy times.

2 Celebrating a New Year is a popular practice both in the East and the West. The celebrations on Vesakha or "Buddha's birthday", on the other hand, recall his birth as well as different stages of his life. While Christmas and Easter are well-known Christian festivals, Ramadan and Eid, which is celebrated at the end of Ramadan, are well-known Islamic ones. Some rituals and festivities are associated with dreams. The Australian Aborigines celebrate the Dream Journey as a mark of their closeness with the land. All religious or cultural communities observe their own rituals and festivities and many of them have done so for thousands of years.

 ISBN-978-81-8477-730-7

Self-expression

A. Read the verse excerpt below. Note that they are the opening lines of a poem by an unknown author.

Sudden swallows swiftly skimming,
Sunset's slowly spreading shade,
Silvery songsters sweetly singing,
Summer's soothing serenade.

B. Discuss what you read with a partner.

1. Did the verse make you feel happy, sad or wistful?
2. What feeling do you think the poet wants to convey?
3. Did you note that the piece has a recurring "s" sound? If so, name the technique used to create this effect.

 ISBN-978-81-8477-730-7

5 Pretty Words

Read the poem below by Elinor Wylie and answer the questions below.

1 Poets make pets of pretty, docile words:
I love smooth words, like gold-
enamelled fish
Which circle slowly with a silken swish,
And tender ones, like downy-feathered
birds:
Words shy and **dappled**, deep-eyed
deer in herds,
Come to my hand, and playful if I
wish,
Or purring softly at a silver dish,
Blue Persian kittens fed on cream
and curds.

2 I love bright words, words up and
singing early;
Words that are **luminous** in the dark,
and sing;

How does the poem change from one verse to the next?

---

enamelled: a layer of protective coating
dappled: spotted, speckled
luminous: glowing, shining

 ISBN-978-81-8477-730-7

Warm lazy words, white cattle under
trees;
I love words **opalescent**, cool, and pearly,
Like midsummer moths, and honied words
like bees,
Gilded and sticky, with a little sting.

Pearl in an oyster

Reading Comprehension

Answer the following questions.

Level 1

1. What do you think purrs softly at a silver dish and why?
2. Apart from words, can you think of other things that may be described as "opalescent, cool, and pearly"?
3. Lots of animals are mentioned in the poem. Can you name them?
4. What are bright words compared to?

Level 2

5. What do you think the poet generally feels about words?
6. Explain why the poet feels this way.
7. What are the various feelings expressed in the poem? Describe three of them, mentioning the words each one is linked to.
8. What words in the poem best appeal to you? Explain your answer.
9. How do you think poets make pets of words?

---

opalescent: white colours that shine

 ISBN-978-81-8477-730-7

Level 3

10. Which expressions in the table below appeal to the various senses of sight, hearing, taste, smell and touch? Write the name of the sense or senses (if you think there is more than one) each expression refers to in the right-hand column of the table.

Image	Sense
purring softly	
silver dish	
Persian kittens	
cream and curds	
opalescent and pearly	

Persian kittens

11. Add two more expressions from the poem to the table above and name the senses they appeal to.

 ISBN-978-81-8477-730-7

12. Is there anything you particularly like about the poem *Pretty Words*? Write a few words about the poet's style.

Vocabulary

Alliteration is the repeated use of a particular letter or sound at the beginning of words or sets of words. It is a commonly used poetic device.

Take a second look at the verse in the previous section.

> **S**udden **s**wallows **s**wiftly **s**kimming,
>
> **S**unset's **s**lowly **s**preading **s**hade,
>
> **S**ilvery **s**ongsters **s**weetly **s**inging,
>
> **S**ummer's **s**oothing **s**erenade.

The "s" sound is repeated at the beginning of every word and hence the verse can be said to be "alliterative".

Sometimes, the recurring letters may appear in positions other than the beginning of words. For example:

The r**ain** in Sp**ain** falls m**ain**ly on the pl**ain**s.

Alliteration is usually used to enhance the sound effect and rhythm of a poem. It also helps to emphasise an idea and support the theme. Apart from poems, alliteration is also used in advertising, leaflets, newspaper headlines and other non-fiction writing that aims to catch instant attention. Commercial organisations often use alliteration to make their brand names memorable. **C**oca-**C**ola, **D**unkin' **D**onuts , **A**merican **A**irlines are some examples.

Identify other examples of alliteration in the poem *Pretty Words*. Answer the following questions.

1. How many examples of alliteration can you find in the first stanza?
2. Choose two examples and say how they affect the overall impact of the poem.

 ISBN-978-81-8477-730-7

Grammar

Words are said to **rhyme** when they have the same sound at the end. The spelling is not always the same for the same sound.

A. Read the verse extract from John Keats' *Ode to a Nightingale* and answer the questions below.

My heart aches, and a drowsy numbness pains
My sense, as though of **hemlock** I had drunk,
Or emptied some dull **opiate** to the drains
One minute past, and **Lethe**-wards had sunk:
'Tis not through envy of thy happy lot,
But being too happy in **thine** happiness,
That **thou**, light-wingèd **Dryad** of the trees,
In some melodious plot
Of beechen green, and shadows numberless,
Singest of summer in full-throated ease.

1. Write down all the rhyming words in the poem.
2. Are the rhyming words spelled the same way?

---

hemlock: a highly poisonous European plant
opiate: a mixture containing opium
Lethe: a mythological river associated with death
thine: your
thou: you
Dryad: a mythological spirit of nature

 ISBN-978-81-8477-730-7

B. Read the poem *Pretty Words* once more. There are several examples of rhymes in it. Write them down.

C. Circle the two words that rhyme best in each line.

1.	double	triple	tunnel	bubble	petal	babble
2.	journey	stormy	boney	Bernie	rainy	hourly
3.	molten	flatten	plankton	cotton	kitten	pattern
4.	broker	trainer	striker	campaigner	plainer	baker
5.	tremendous	arduous	adventurous	stupendous	anxious	

D. Think of two rhyming words for each of the words in the table. The first rhyme should spell the same. The second should spell different. An example is done for you.

Word	Rhyme spelled the same	Rhyme spelled differently
fair	stair	bear
door		
beach		
tower		
port		
bought		
pretence		
declare		

 ISBN-978-81-8477-730-7

Listening

Close your eyes as you listen to the poem. What pictures do you see? What sounds do you hear? How does the poem make you feel? Write down the answers of the following questions.

1. What does the poem say about how beasts are treated? How does it contrast with the way the sacred cow is treated in India? Jot down at least three points of contrast in the table below.

How beasts are treated in Kipling's poem	How the sacred cow is treated in India

2. Why do you think the beasts are wise? Mention words from the poem to support what you say.

 ISBN-978-81-8477-730-7

Speaking

Read the poem *The Crocodile* by Lewis Carroll aloud and answer the questions.

The Crocodile

How **doth** the little crocodile
  Improve his shining tail,
And pour the waters of the **Nile**
  On every golden scale!

How cheerfully he seems to grin,
  How neatly spreads his claws,
And welcomes little fishes in
  With gently smiling jaws!

1. Is the poem humorous, thoughtful or sad? What do you like most about the poem?
2. What would be the most effective way of presenting the poem to a group? In what tone and pace would you read? Prepare carefully and make a presentation to a group of three or four students.

---

doth: does
Nile: a river that runs through Egypt and many other countries in Africa

 ISBN-978-81-8477-730-7

Writing

In the poem *Pretty Words*, the poet has used several compound words to give a lifelike feel to words. Look at the table below for examples.

A. Add compound words describing other creatures and complete the table taking your cue from the examples.

Type of words	Creatures
smooth words	gold-enamelled fish
tender words	downy-feathered birds
shy words	deep-eyed deer
comic words	
sad words	
angry words	
jolly words	

B. Describe briefly a visit to the zoo, using some of the compound words from the table to describe the creatures you saw.

Activity

Kennings are devices used in Old Norse poetry. Old Norse poetry was written hundreds of years ago by poets living in the Arctic countries such as Iceland and Norway. A kenning is a compound word that describes the nature or feel of what it denotes.

 ISBN-978-81-8477-730-7

Two examples are given below.

A boat could be called a "wind-billower".

A seabird could be a "foam-winger".

A kenning describes one thing in terms of another and is thus often considered similar to a metaphor.

Write a poem about an animal with the help of a series of at least six kennings. Follow the steps below.

1. Choose the animal you would like to write about.
2. List its various traits in the first column of a table like the one below.
3. Using the list, create ideas for your poem and note them down in the next column. Construct kennings from what you have jotted down.

An example is given below.

Animal: Dog		
Traits	**Ideas for kennings**	**Kennings**
noisy	related to a dog's bark	woof-wagger

4. Complete your poem and read it out to a partner. Ask your partner to read out his or her kennings too.

 ISBN-978-81-8477-730-7

6 Matilda

Read the excerpt from *Matilda* by Roald Dahl.

1 It's a funny thing about mothers and fathers. Even when their own child is the most disgusting little blister you could ever imagine, they still think he or she is wonderful.

2 Some parents go further. They become so blinded by adoration they manage to convince themselves their child has the qualities of a genius.

3 Well, there is nothing very wrong with all this. It's the way of the world. It is only when parents begin telling us about the brilliance of their own revolting offspring, that we start shouting, "Bring us a basin! We're going to be sick!"

4 School teachers suffer a good deal from having to listen to this sort of **twaddle** from proud parents, but they usually get their own back when the time comes to write the end-of-term reports. If I were a teacher I would cook up some real scorchers for the children of doting parents. "Your son Maximilian," I would write, "is a total wash-out. I hope you have a family business you can push him into when he leaves school because he sure as heck won't get a job anywhere else." Or if I were feeling lyrical that day, I might write, "It is a curious truth that grasshoppers have their hearing organs in the side of their abdomen. Your daughter Vanessa, judging by what she's learned this term, has no hearing organs at all."

What style does the author use to address the reader?

5 I might even delve deeper into natural history and say, "The periodical cicada spends six years as a grub underground, and no more than six days as a free creature of sunlight and air. Your son Wilfred has spent six years as a grub in this school and we are still waiting for him to emerge

---

twaddle: nonsensical talk or writing

 ISBN-978-81-8477-730-7

from the chrysalis." A particularly poisonous little girl might sting me into saying, "Fiona has the same glacial beauty as an iceberg, but unlike the iceberg she has absolutely nothing below the surface." I think I might enjoy writing end-of-term reports for the stinkers in my class. But enough of that. We have to get on.

6 Occasionally one comes across parents who take the opposite line, who show no interest at all in their children, and these of course are far worse than the doting ones. Mr and Mrs Wormwood were two such parents. They had a son called Michael and a daughter called Matilda, and the parents looked upon Matilda in particular as nothing more than a scab. A scab is something you have to put up with until the time comes when you can pick it off and flick it away. Mr and Mrs Wormwood looked forward enormously to the time when they could pick their little daughter off and flick her away, preferably into the next country or even further than that.

Reading Comprehension

Answer the following questions.

Level 1

1. Who is "blinded by adoration" in the above passage?
2. Who, according to the author, suffer "a good deal" from parents' attitudes towards their children?
3. When do these suffering people get their own back?
4. To what does the author compare Vanessa, Wilfred and Fiona? Briefly mention what the author says about each of them in the table below.

Vanessa	Wilfred	Fiona

 ISBN-978-81-8477-730-7

5. What are the names of the parents the author considers an exception and what are their children called?

Level 2

6. How, according to the author, are parents commonly inclined towards their children?
7. What is the author's opinion about them?
8. What does the author mean when he says Vanessa "has no hearing organs at all"?
9. What does the author mean by the expression "glacial beauty"?
10. What is natural history? How does the author use it?
11. Who do you think the author will choose as the main character as he unfolds the story? How do you know?

Level 3

12. Scan the excerpt and find the specific information that can help you answer the six questions on the next page. Set a time limit for yourself. You can use any of the following methods for scanning.

- Skipping words in a sentence.

- Scanning down the middle of the page.

- Scanning a paragraph up and down from left to right.

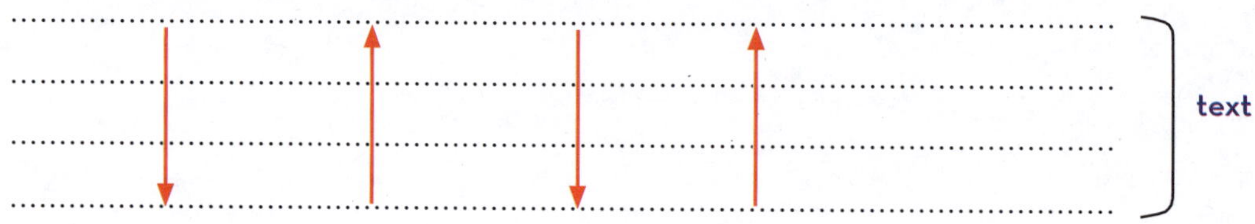

 ISBN-978-81-8477-730-7

a) Who are described as "disgusting little blisters"?

b) Who, according to the author, is "a total wash-out"?

c) Where are hearing organs located on a grasshopper's body?

d) Which creature spends six years as a grub?

e) Who, according to the author, behaves like a grub?

f) Who is looked upon as a scab? By whom?

Vocabulary

Roald Dahl appears to have adopted a predominantly chatty and humorous style in writing the story. The frequent use of **humorous images and expressions** is an indicator.

For example, the similarity drawn between a spoilt child and a "disgusting little blister" is overtly funny.

A. Find three more expressions in the excerpt that tickle your funny bone.

B. Together with a partner, write down some humorous descriptions for the following.

1. Someone startled by the burst of a balloon.
2. A small child whose face is smeared with sticky candy or chocolate.
3. A jumper knitted by a relative, which is three times your size.

C. Read out your descriptions to your partner and listen to the ones he or she has written.

 ISBN-978-81-8477-730-7

Grammar

A **linking verb** joins the subject of a sentence with a word or set of words containing information about the subject. The word or set of words containing information is called a **complement**.

linking verb — complement

subject — Jimmy **is** a great table-tennis player.

This piece of information is about the subject Jimmy.

Look at the sentence below.

Jimmy **plays** great table tennis.

The verb "plays" is an **action verb** and not a linking verb. It is not followed by information about the subject and is therefore not a complement.

A. Decide whether the verbs in the following sentences are linking verbs or action verbs. Tick the correct column for each sentence.

Sentence	Linking verb	Action verb
The cat yawned sleepily.		
She never tidies her room.		
She is a very good pianist.		
They were early yesterday.		
The dog trotted along happily.		
The leaves turn yellow in autumn.		
I am happy for you.		
He became concerned about the traffic.		

 ISBN-978-81-8477-730-7

B. Compose one sentence containing a linking verb and one an action verb.

C. Underline the subjects and circle the verbs in these sentences.

1. They blew the trumpets.
2. The water is a beautiful, clear blue.
3. The crowd cheered and clapped with joy.
4. Mark laid his book on the desk.
5. Mum forgot to water my plants!
6. Sanjay closed the door quietly and walked over to the table.

D. Complete these sentences using the linking verbs in the box correctly.

am	is	are	was	were	became	seems

1. The tower of the castle ...
2. The marathon ...
3. The fir trees ...
4. I ...
5. Ali and Jacob ...
6. Krishna ...
7. The thought ...

E. Complete these sentences using an action verb of your own choice. Try to choose interesting verbs.

1. The horse _________________ along the dusty path towards the gate.
2. Please _________________ my gym bag, which is in the hall.

 ISBN-978-81-8477-730-7

3. Sally's hamster and gerbil ________________ together.

4. The wind ________________ so hard we could barely get out the door.

5. I ________________ if we could go to the movies tomorrow?

Listening

Listen to the excerpt from *Matilda* and answer the questions below.

1. What is Matilda like?
2. Describe two of Mr and Mrs Wormwood's character traits.
3. Did Mr and Mrs Wormwood ignore their daughter? Give reasons to support your answer.
4. What is Michael like?

Speaking

Prepare a short talk for your partner. Choose your topic from the options below. Ask your partner to prepare a talk on the topic other than the one you choose. Listen to your partner's speech, and then make your own presentation.

1. Present a talk about Matilda highlighting her character traits.
2. Present a talk on Mr and Mrs Wormwood focussing on their character traits.

 ISBN-978-81-8477-730-7

Writing

Try and write a few paragraphs adopting a style similar to that of Roald Dahl. Follow the steps below.

1. Read the following.

   A native of the British Isles, the hazel dormouse has large black eyes and golden fur. Its body is no more than a few inches long. You may remember that the dormouse in the Lewis Carroll tale *Alice in Wonderland* was so small it could sleep in a teapot. The hazelnut dormouse feeds on a wide variety of fruit, nuts, plants and insects and can be found mostly in hedgerows and woodland.

   The hazelnut dormouse is so called because of its unique habits. Sleep is one of its main preoccupations and it fattens up before hibernation by eating hazelnuts. During the month of October, when the days begin to get colder and shorter, the dormouse takes to its bed - usually beneath fallen leaves and twigs where it is warm. There it sleeps until the months of April and May.

   When it wakes up, it starts weaving a nest from twigs, green leaves and bark. The females raise their litter in their nests during the months of July or August and all through the summer dormice take frequent naps.

2. Take your cue from the above passage and compose a humorous paragraph on a pet cat. Follow the steps below.

   - Think of all the things the cat could have in common with a dormouse. Concentrate on its appearance and behaviour.
   - List your points in the chart below.
   - Use the points to write the paragraph. If you so need, you can use the following words to help you begin.

   Did you know that the hazelnut dormouse...?
   My cat...

 ISBN-978-81-8477-730-7

Similarities between dormouse and pet cat	
Dormouse	**Pet cat**

3. Now write your own humorous piece, unaided, about any one of the following topics.
   - A friendly giraffe at a safari park
   - A llama that has stolen your mother's best gloves
   - A hippopotamus yawning

 ISBN-978-81-8477-730-7

Activity

A **blurb**, found on the back cover of a book, is a brief hint about its content. It is usually just a paragraph long and aims to attract the buyer.

A. Make a small group and write a blurb for the back cover of *Matilda*.

Remember

Dos and don'ts to keep in mind while writing a blurb:

Dos

- Write your blurb in a way that attracts the reader.
- Give information on the main characters, indicating what they are like and what problems they may have to face.

Don'ts

- Ensure you present only an outline of the beginning of the story. Do not give away too much of the plot.
- Do not disclose the ending!

B. Read the blurbs written by the other group members. Which do you think is the best blurb? Why?

 ISBN-978-81-8477-730-7

Theme 4

The Natural World

A. Look at the picture. What does it show?

1. Can you spot the planet Earth in the picture?
2. Name the planet which has rings around it.
3. What is the smaller body outside the ring of planets?

B. Answer the following questions.

1. Name the eight planets in the picture or find out their names in case you don't know.
2. Which planet is nearest to the Sun?
3. Which planet is often referred to as the "red planet"?
4. There are now only eight planets in the solar system instead of nine. Which planet was removed from the list? Do you know why?

 ISBN-978-81-8477-730-7

7 Science Star Omar

Read the following excerpt taken from the book *Suffering Scientists* by Nick Arnold, an author best known for his Horrible Science series of books. It is about Ghiyath al-Din Abu-l'Fath Umar ibn Ibrahim Al-Nisaburi al-Khayyami, better known as Omar Khayyam.

1 Omar Khayyam (AD 1048–1131) was born in Khorasan in Persia, now known as Iran. Nothing is known about his family but the name Khayyami means "tent maker", so maybe that's what his family did for a living. Young Omar must have had a good education because he became a teacher with an interest in scientific subjects. But he found it hard to study. He later admitted that as a teacher, he was so busy teaching, he had little time to find out about the subject he was supposed to be telling children about. Does your teacher have this problem – and dare you ask?

? What do you know about Omar from this paragraph?

2 At least Omar managed to find time to write a book on algebra and another on music. Given a bit longer he might have written a book on musical maths!

Around 1070 Omar made friends with an important judge Abu Tahir. The judge must have been into maths because Omar dedicated two more books on algebra to him.

3 Omar's work for the judge attracted the attention of the Sultan Jalal al-Din. And the Sultan gave Omar the job of looking after his astronomical observatory.

4 Omar was very happy and he spent the next eighteen years tracking the movements of over 100 stars. And this is how he made his crucial calendar.

? What were two of Omar's main interests?

 ISBN-978-81-8477-730-7

5 Seen from the earth, the stars seem to move around us during the year. By 1079 Omar had enough information from his stargazing to calculate the exact length of a year.

6 In fact, he was just 0.0002 days wrong. This meant that if you followed a calendar drawn up by Omar, you'd find it was one day out in 5,000 years. Mind you, by then you might be too old to care too much even if you ended up missing your birthday or eating Christmas pudding on Boxing Day! (Our present calendar is actually less accurate than Omar's because it loses one day in 3,333 years.)

7 Omar advised the Sultan to rejig the calendar to fit in with his newly calculated year. But then things began to go wrong.

8 First, the Sultan died.

9 Omar thought things could carry on because he was a pal of the Grand Vizier – the **Persian** Prime Minister.

10 But the Sultan's queen seized power. She quarrelled with the Vizier and he was murdered by a mysterious killer.

11 Any friend of the Vizier wasn't exactly flavour of the month with the queen. Omar's observatory was closed down.

12 Omar wrote a book claiming that the ancient rulers of Persia were really nice people. They were kind-hearted and generous – especially to astronomers like Omar.

Persian: Iranian; Iran was once called Persia

13 But the queen was definitely not amused by this unsubtle hint and not surprisingly Omar was never given another job.

14 One of Omar's jobs was to draw up horoscopes based on the positions of the stars to foretell the future for important people. He wasted loads of time on this even though he secretly didn't believe in it. (Of course, people still believe in this practice, known as astrology, but you'd never catch a modern scientist peeping at their horoscope in the paper.)

Bet you never knew!

Omar was an excellent poet and he is better known in Europe for his verse, rather than for his study of the universe.

The *Rubaiyat of Omar Khayyam*, a translation of Omar's poems by the famous British poet Edward FitzGerald, is one of his most well-known works. The poems are small, mostly consisting of quatrains, and speak of love, beauty, mystery and freedom of thought.

 ISBN-978-81-8477-730-7

Reading Comprehension

Answer the following questions.

Level 1

1. What is Omar's second name?
2. What is Omar's nationality?
3. When was Omar born and when did he die?
4. What do we know about Omar's family?
5. What profession did Omar first take up?
6. What were the two subjects Omar wrote about early in his career?
7. Who was the judge Omar became friends with?

Level 2

8. Was Omar an honest person? Give reasons to support your answer.
9. In what way did the judge make a difference to Omar's life?
10. What important calculation did Omar make and how do you think he felt about it?
11. The author says Omar wasn't quite right about the length of a year but that it didn't matter much. Why do you think the author says so?
12. What was the series of important events that affected Omar's later career and how?
13. How did Omar try to influence the queen? Was he successful?

 ISBN-978-81-8477-730-7

Level 3

14. Scan the passage and find all the important dates concerning Omar Khayyam's life. They may be important occasions (such as his date of birth) or major events that affected his life (such as the death of the Sultan). If you do not know the exact date, give an approximate one.

15. Using the dates you have listed, chalk out Omar Khayyam's timeline. Try to give information on at least eight dates.

Omar Khayyam's timeline

Events

Vocabulary

Synonyms are words that have the same or almost the same meaning. For example, "**buy**" and "**purchase**". Words that mean more or less the same are said to be **synonymous** with each other. For example, "**happy**" and "**elated**" are synonymous. Note that a word may have two different meanings and that its synonym may refer to only one of those meanings. For example, "student" is a synonym for "pupil" only when the latter does not stand for the aperture (pupil) in the eye. The words listed in the table below are all taken from the passage *Science Star Omar*.

 ISBN-978-81-8477-730-7

A. Find the words listed below in the passage. Think of a synonym for each (without using a thesaurus) and write it down in the right-hand column.

B. Check your answer with the help of a thesaurus and add another synonym for each one.

Word	Synonym
chapter	
fortunately	
education	
teacher	
problem	
important	
attention	
information	
accurate	
quarrelled	

C. Many words lose their efficacy due to overuse. "Nice" is one of them. How many synonyms can you think of that can be used in place of "nice"?

 ISBN-978-81-8477-730-7

D. Rewrite the following paragraph from Science Star Omar, replacing the underlined words with suitable synonyms. You can use more than one word if you need to.

One of Omar's jobs was to draw up horoscopes based on the positions of the stars to foretell the future for important people. He wasted loads of time on this even though he secretly didn't believe in it. (Of course, people still believe in this practice, known as astrology, but you'd never catch a modern scientist peeping at their horoscope in the paper.)

E. Think of two synonyms for these words without looking in a thesaurus or dictionary and write them down.

1. jump
2. fly
3. lamp
4. climb
5. recall
6. organise

F. Match these words with their synonyms correctly.

Word	Synonym
manufacture	crack
imperfect	respect
erode	make
squander	custom
outcome	wear away
homage	misuse
crevice	result
rite	faulty

 ISBN-978-81-8477-730-7

G. Think of a synonym to replace the words in bold.

My **little** sister began secondary school last week, but she had no **inclination** to go at all. She thought the building was old and **ugly**, the playground too large and **uninviting** and the teachers and **students** very **unfriendly**. By the **end** of the first week we couldn't get her to come home. She loved it so much!

Grammar

A **coordinating conjunction** is a word that links the different thoughts, ideas and information within a sentence. It usually occurs in the middle of a sentence. Examples of coordinating conjunctions are "**and**", "**but**", "**so**", "**or**" and "**yet**".

Omar Khayyam was a scientist **and** a poet.

The coordinating conjunction "and" links two ideas together – Omar was a scientist and Omar was also a poet.

A. Join the sentence pairs with suitable coordinating conjunctions from the box below.

and	but	so	or	yet

1. Omar was born in Iran. We do not know anything about his family.
2. Omar Khayyam was interested in science. He became a teacher.
3. He did not find it easy to study. He became a great scholar.
4. He wrote a book about mathematics. He wrote another book about music.
5. Omar was busy teaching. He could not do as much research as he needed to.

 ISBN-978-81-8477-730-7

6. He studied the stars with dedication. He amassed information.
7. Omar wanted to present his calendar to the Sultan. He would probably have waited for the Sultan to inquire about it first.

B. In which of the above sentences can you use more than one coordinating conjunction? Discuss the question with a friend, focusing on how the meaning of the sentence would change with such an addition.

C. Fill in the blanks with suitable conjunctions.

1. Hurry up ________________ you will be late.
2. I went to the market ________________ bought some vegetables.
3. She cannot attend the meeting ________________ she is too busy.
4. We were getting tired ________________ we stopped for a rest.
5. He had to retire ________________ of ill health.

D. Complete these pairs of sentences. Then discuss with a partner how the meaning changes with the change of conjunction in each sentence pair.

1. They found the keys but ...

   They found the keys so ...
2. She would feed the fish in the tank and ...

   She would feed the fish in the tank or ...
3. The day had finally arrived for ...

   The day had finally arrived yet ...

 ISBN-978-81-8477-730-7

E. All the conjunctions in the box are linked to time. The first has been used in the sentence below. Continue with the sentence and compose a paragraph about what all Sandeep did, using the remaining conjunctions.

at	before	next	then	after	finally

Sandeep got home **at** four o'clock and threw his bag on the chair...

F. Complete these sentences using a conjunction of your own choice.

1. Harry was unhappy about the homework he had to do ...
2. The bike was left outside the door ...
3. He was washing the dishes ...
4. She looked after her baby brother ...
5. Pedro could not find his mobile ...

Listening

Listen to the information on planets in the solar system and answer the questions below.

1. Which planet is called the Morning Star or the Evening Star?
2. Point out one similarity between Venus and Earth.
3. What features does the planet Mars have?
4. Which is the largest planet in our solar system?
5. What is the Great Red Spot?
6. Which other planets, apart from the one mentioned, are made of gas?

 ISBN-978-81-8477-730-7

Speaking

Present a short talk to a group, comparing and contrasting Venus and Jupiter. Keep the following guidelines in mind.

1. Try not to read from your notes or to use them as a prompt.
2. Note down the main differences between the planets and memorise them first.
3. Use what you have learnt as a mental guide when you are speaking.

Venus

Jupiter

Writing

Write a short biography of Omar Khayyam according to the guidelines below.

1. Use the following data.
   - The information contained in the passage *Science Star Omar*
   - The timeline you created (ensuring that it is accurate)
2. With your teacher's guidance, carry out further research using the library or the Internet.

 ISBN-978-81-8477-730-7

3. Make a character sheet like the one below and use it as a guide to sketch Omar's character.

Omar Khayyam	**Notes**
Essential facts (such as, where he was born)	
His occupations and the places where he lived and worked	
Brief outline of his life (chain of main events and important people he knew)	
Work that he carried out in different fields (such as science and literature)	
His contribution to world knowledge	
Any other information	

4. Think of a suitable title for your biography. You can make a colourful booklet out of your biography and include pictures and sketches in it.
5. Share your biography with your partner and assess each other's work.

 ISBN-978-81-8477-730-7

Activity

Different parts of the world use different kinds of calendars for different reasons.

Research and create a fact file about calendars. Organise your fact file into various sections according to the information you have. Here are some ideas, but feel free to draw up your own.

Types of Calendar	Calendar fact file
Gregorian Calendar	
Lunar Calendar	
Indian National Calendar	
Omar Khayyam's calendar	
Dates important to me	

 ISBN-978-81-8477-730-7

8 Plates on the Crust

Read the excerpt from the explanatory text *Earthquake* by Fred Martin.

The Earth's Layers

1 The Earth's hard outer layer is called "crust". Extending only from 5 to 50 km deep, it is remarkably thin compared to the 6,000 km spanning the Earth's surface and its centre.

2 About 30 years ago, geologists discovered that the crust is not one solid piece. Instead, it is split into separate slabs that are now commonly referred to as "plates". The plates float like giant rafts one on top of the lowermost layer. The crust and upper part of the **mantle**, which is the layer immediately below the crust, together form the lithosphere.

What do "plates" refer to?

3 About 300 million years ago, there was only one large continent that geologists call Pangaea. Gradually the continent began to break up into separate plates. Since then the plates have been moving about in all directions. Places that were once near the equator are now much further north. The fact helps to explain why limestone containing coral fossils is found in places where it is now far too cold for coral to grow.

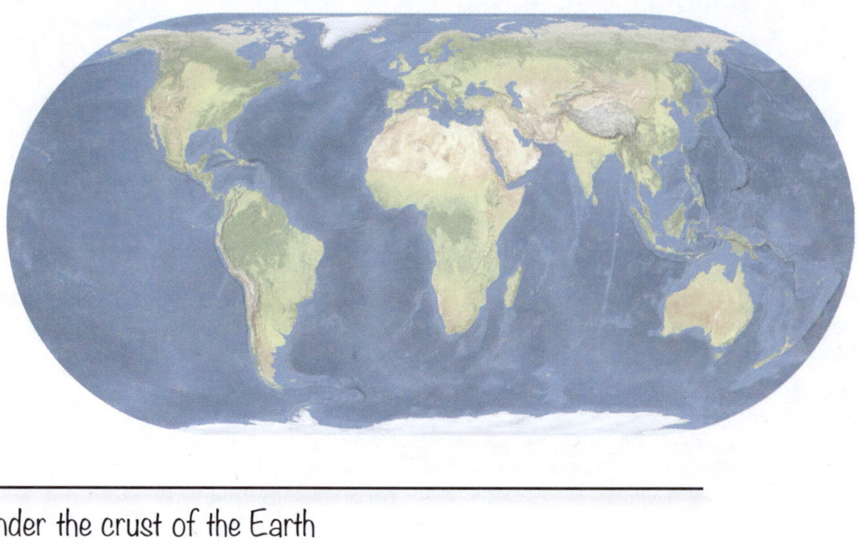

mantle: section under the crust of the Earth

 ISBN-978-81-8477-730-7

4 The crust now has about fifteen large plates and several smaller ones. They move very slowly – about 2–4 cm every year. This does not seem fast to us, but geological time is measured against millions of years. Geologists, going by their own calculations, believe that the speed is strong enough to open up an ocean 2,000 km wide in about 50 million years. In fact, the Atlantic Ocean has opened up in this kind of a time frame. It is thus evident why some of the older rocks, such as coal, are found to be of the same kind on both sides of the Atlantic Ocean.

How many plates are there now?

Why the Plates Move

5 It is quite evident that a phenomenon is taking place inside the Earth and shifting the plates around. It is hard to find out the exact nature of this phenomenon as it is not possible for anyone to go that deep inside. The molten rock thrown up by volcanoes contains clues about what may lie deep under the crust. Shock waves from earthquakes also give indications about the inside of the Earth.

Why is it difficult to know how plates move?

Augustine Volcano, Alaska

6 The inside of the Earth is so hot that rocks tend to melt and flow. However, they remain partially solid and move only very slowly because of the intense pressure all around. Currents of hot material move towards the crust from inside the mantle. When they reach the mantle, they separate under the crust and flow along in different directions. These streams of hot molten material are called convection currents. The convection currents in the rocks

 ISBN-978-81-8477-730-7

push the plates above them and set them moving. As the plates move, they crash into each other, move away or slide past each other. The pressures that cause these movements are enormous and cannot be stopped.

7 The plates move slowly, grinding against each other and sending out vibrations through the rocks. These vibrations are felt on the ground as tremors.

8 Sometimes, parts of the plates get locked into each other and stop moving for a while. On such occasions, the pressure to move keeps building up until the plates jolt forward again. All the energy is suddenly released and there is a major earthquake.

Destruction caused by earthquake

Reading Comprehension

Answer the following questions.

Level 1

1. What do you understand by the Earth's "crust"? How deep is it?
2. How different is the present-day crust from what it was 300 million years ago?

 ISBN-978-81-8477-730-7

3. What is the term used to refer to the Earth's outer layer?

4. What are the Earth's "plates" and "mantle"?

5. What have you learnt about the movement of the plates?

6. Why do rocks inside the Earth melt?

7. How are convection currents formed? How do they affect the Earth?

8. What do you know about locked plates?

Level 2

9. What kind of temperature do coral need for growth?

10. Why are fossils of coral found in the northern countries?

11. What is the difference between time as we know it and geological time?

12. What causes plates to move? What effect does this movement have?

13. Do you think locked plates are dangerous? Why?

Level 3

14. The above passage has many sentences sharing a cause and effect relationship. Explain the relationship between the two statements (**a** and **b**) below. Indicate which of them contains the cause and which the effect.

a) Since then the plates have been moving about in all directions.

b) Places that were once near the equator are now much further north.

15. Complete the flow diagram, bringing out the cause and effect relationship between the words in the statements below.

- The inside of the Earth is so hot that rocks tend to melt.

Cause	⇨	**Effect**

 ISBN-978-81-8477-730-7

- They (the rocks) remain partially solid and move only very slowly because of the intense pressure all around.

Cause	⇨	**Effect**

- The convection currents in the rocks push the plates above them and as a result the plates start moving.

Cause	⇨	**Effect**

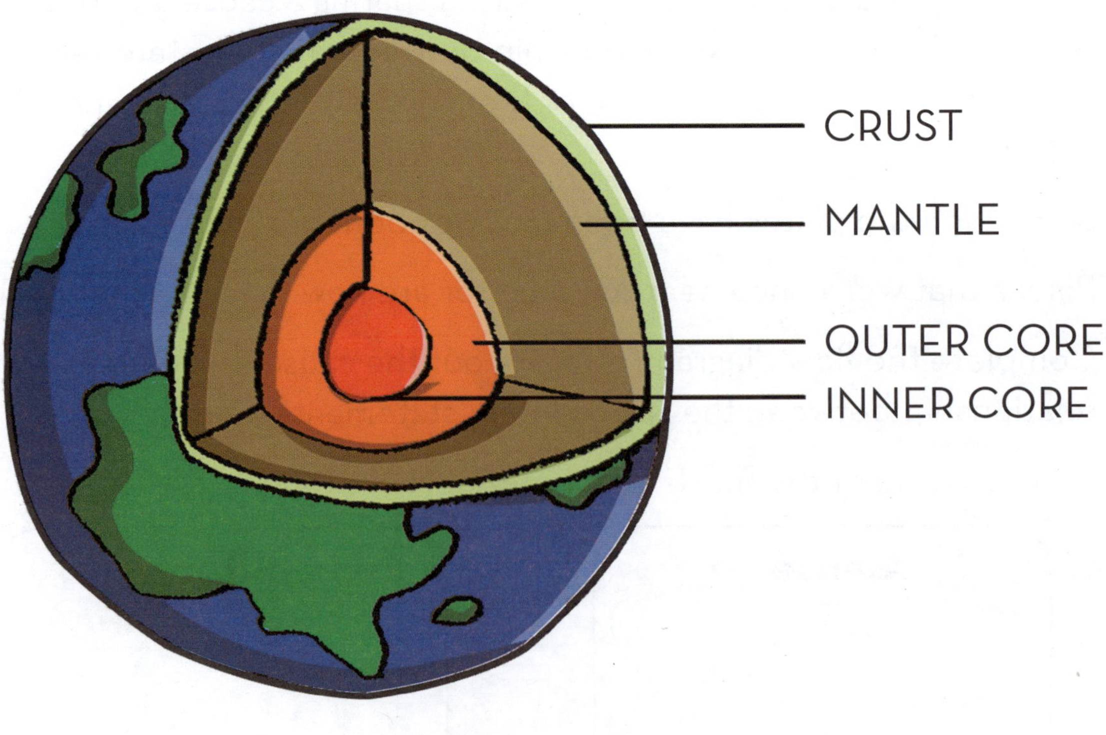

 ISBN-978-81-8477-730-7

Vocabulary

The cause and effect relationship between parts of a sentence is indicated by certain words that are termed **causal connectors**. Some examples of casual connectors are given in the box below.

cause	because	since so	thus	consequently
in consequence	therefore	as a result	resulting	effect

A. Join the following sets of sentences using suitable causal connectors. You can create more than one sentence with a single set.

1. Over millions of years the plates moved further apart. The Atlantic Ocean opened up.
2. The dolphin has a smooth curved shape. It moves rapidly through water.
3. Rain falls. Clouds become saturated with water droplets.
4. The dodo is extinct. It was a very large flightless bird. It was very easy for humans to hunt.

 ISBN-978-81-8477-730-7

B. Fill in the blanks with causal connectors, using a different connector in each blank. Read through the paragraph before you begin.

As fast as they could they climbed up the steep bank _____ there was no other way to go _____ the road was blocked at either end. The full moon slipped from behind a cloud, _____ they threw themselves on the wet earth under the old oak tree for fear of being seen. _____ Polly's dress was covered in dirt and Jack's white trainers turned a muddy brown. They stayed as still as they could for several minutes. _____ they were soaked through, but at least the guards had not caught them.

C. Rewrite each pair of sentences by adding a causal connector to it. You can also join them to form single sentences. Use different connectors each time and make sure to change the punctuation in case you join up the sentences.

1. She left her bag on the train.
   She had no money to get home.
2. He designed the perfect computer game.
   He won several awards.
3. Jackie loved skiing.
   She skied as often as she could.
4. We did not win the race.
   We have to accept it.

Grammar

The **present tense** is a way of describing something that is going on at the time of speaking.

I exercise every day.

When we refer to something that happened in the past we use the **past tense**.

We won the last cricket match.

 ISBN-978-81-8477-730-7

A. Underline the verbs in the present tense in the following paragraph.

The crust now has about fifteen large plates and several smaller ones. They move very slowly – about 2–4 cm every year. This may not seem fast to us, but geological time is measured in the context of millions of years.

Geologists, going by their own calculations, believe that the speed is strong enough to open up an ocean 2,000 km wide in about 50 million years. In fact, the Atlantic Ocean has opened up in this kind of a time frame. It is thus evident why some of the older rocks, such as coal, are found to be of the same kind on both sides of the Atlantic Ocean.

B. Underline the verbs in the past tense in the following sentences.

1. About 30 years ago, geologists discovered that the crust is not one solid piece.
2. About 300 million years ago, there was only one large continent.
3. Gradually the continents began to break into separate plates.

C. Read the sentences in the table and follow the instructions below.

1. Decide which tense each sentence is written in. Tick the correct column.
2. Convert each sentence into the other tense and write it in the table.
3. Use the apostrophe where you can.

Example	Present tense	Past tense
I'm sorry.		
It's true.		
We'd already done it!		
He'd played well.		
You're sure?		
They're fine.		
You'd written it?		
It's over!		

 ISBN-978-81-8477-730-7

D. Write the following paragraph in the present tense first. Then write it in the past tense. Before you begin writing, underline the words to be changed.

I'll plan everything very carefully. First I'll buy the best ingredients. Then Mum will show me how to prepare the vegetables and spices. I'll ask Dad to help too. He'll be happy to show me how to cook the rice. Timing will be important, so I'll take advice from Mum again. That'll be how I make a nourishing evening meal.

E. What is wrong with this informative text? Why does it sound odd? Correct it to suit the kind of text it is.

Many natural disasters occurred each year, from volcanic eruptions to earthquakes to avalanches. We forgot how unpredictable and violent the Earth was and it was only when such disasters hit the headlines that we realised how much we were at the mercy of nature.

Listening

Listen to the explanation and answer the following questions.

1. What is the Earth's axis?
2. How long does it take the Earth to spin round once?
3. How do we have day and night?
4. How does the Earth spin round the Sun?
5. How long does it take the Earth to orbit the Sun?

 ISBN-978-81-8477-730-7

Speaking

Choose one topic given below and explain it to your partner. Make sure you understand the topic thoroughly before you begin.

1. What causes night and day?
2. How does the Earth move round the Sun?
3. What is an earthquake and how does it happen?
4. How is a volcano formed? Name a few famous volcanoes.
5. Describe the process by which continents were formed.

Writing

The Richter scale helps scientists study earthquakes. Given below is an image of the Richter scale. Find out more about this instrument. Answer the questions below.

1. Write a short note on the following.
    - How it works
    - Who invented it and when

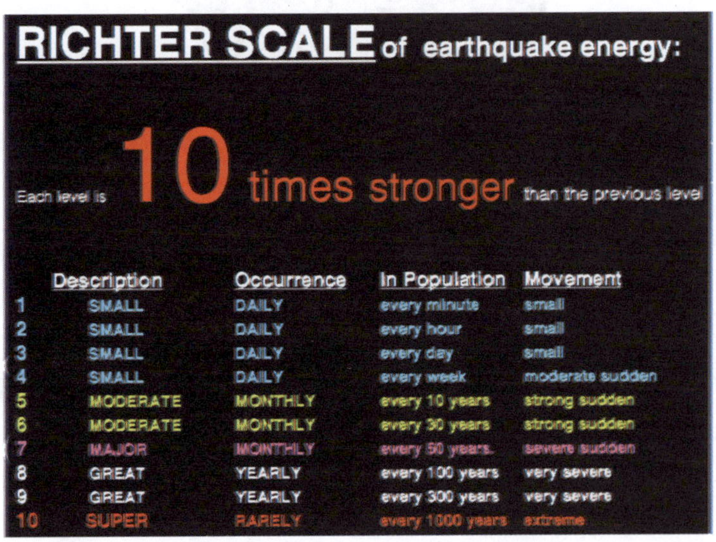
RICHTER SCALE of earthquake energy:

Each level is 10 times stronger than the previous level

	Description	Occurrence	In Population	Movement
1	SMALL	DAILY	every minute	small
2	SMALL	DAILY	every hour	small
3	SMALL	DAILY	every day	small
4	SMALL	DAILY	every week	moderate sudden
5	MODERATE	MONTHLY	every 10 years	strong sudden
6	MODERATE	MONTHLY	every 30 years	strong sudden
7	MAJOR	MONTHLY	every 50 years.	severe sudden
8	GREAT	YEARLY	every 100 years	very severe
9	GREAT	YEARLY	every 300 years	very severe
10	SUPER	RARELY	every 1000 years	extreme

 ISBN-978-81-8477-730-7

2. Design a table on the Richter scale. Your heading should include the following.
    - The time and location of the earthquake
    - The magnitude of the earthquake
    - Its impact, in terms of the approximate extent of destruction
3. Add a glossary, giving information on uncommon or technical words such as "seismic".

Activity

Find out how earthquakes happen. Now, do the following exercises.

1. Study the diagram below. It shows a cross section of the Earth.

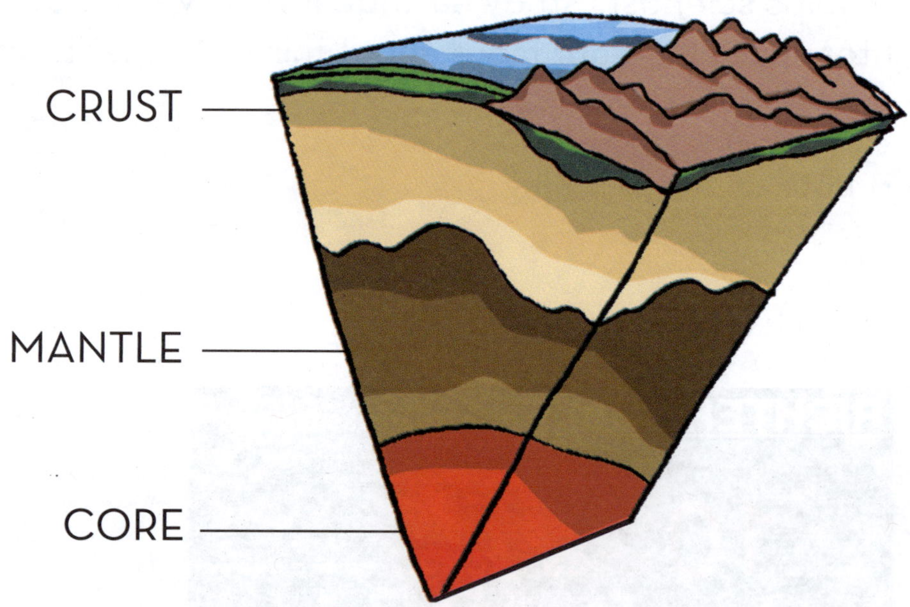

2. Create your own diagram to show how earthquakes happen. Follow the guidelines below.
    - Label the diagram to show its specific parts.
    - Add annotations (written explanations) on how an earthquake happens.

 ISBN-978-81-8477-730-7

Theme 5

The Community

A. Look at the picture.

1. What has happened to all the people?
2. How do you think they are feeling?

B. Answer the following questions.

1. What festival does it depict?
2. What does its name mean?
3. Who celebrates this festival?
4. When is the festival held?
5. What is the significance of the festival?

 ISBN-978-81-8477-730-7

9 India, a Community

Read the following passage by Mary Green.

What are all the things the word "community" stands for?

1 When we think of the word "community", we usually think of our immediate surroundings, of our family and friends or of our neighbourhood. But we can also think of "community" in a much broader sense. We all belong to the human community for instance, and today we are connected to each other across the world in ways that were unimaginable a hundred years ago. The World Wide Web has allowed us all to become closer.

2 We can also think of ourselves as belonging to a nation, however large that nation may be. India is a huge and diverse country, with over a billion people, rich and poor. It is a vast area of land bordered by the Indian Ocean, the Arabian Sea and the Bay of Bengal. In the north are the Himalayas, the "Land of Snow" that borders China and other parts of Asia, an extraordinary chain of mountains in which the famous Mount Everest sits. By contrast, the interior of India is hot, very hot. There are many weather patterns in this enormous country, which has mountains, desert regions, plains and rainforests.

Mt. Everest

 ISBN-978-81-8477-730-7

3 At one time India was not an independent nation. It was a collection of separate kingdoms. Many people came to India as invaders, settlers or traders and became part of the mix. One of the earliest civilisations in India and one of the oldest in the world was the Indus Valley Civilisation. Highly sophisticated, the Indus people built complex cities that had thousands of inhabitants. Later came the Aryans from the north. They not only dominated India for approximately 700 years but also laid the foundations for several religions. Later still came the Persian kings, and the Greeks under **Alexander the Great**. In the modern era India was "the jewel in the crown" of the British Empire. When the British left, India became an independent nation in 1947.

Who were the invaders and settlers in India?

Indian National Flag on the Red Fort

4 Out of India's history came its many languages and festivals as well as its religions. There is Diwali, Ramadan, Parkash Utsav, Wesak, Christmas and the harvest festivals of Pongal in Tamil Nadu and Onam in Kerala, not forgetting the celebrations that take place on August 15, Independence Day – and so many others!

Alexander the Great: a king in ancient Greece who created a large empire

 ISBN-978-81-8477-730-7

5 So what unites such a varied nation? Is it India's festivals and fairs and its hospitality? Is it India's national symbols – the Sarnath lion, the tiger, the lotus flower? Is it the great river Ganges? Perhaps it is India's very diversity, in which people happily belong to individual regions, yet at the same time see themselves as part of a whole, as part of this immense country. What do you think?

Reading Comprehension

Answer the following questions.

Level 1

1. Name the seas and oceans bordering India?
2. Name the most famous mountain of the Himalayas?
3. What does "Land of Snow" refer to? Where is it located?
4. Who were the first people inhabiting India?
5. For how long did the Aryans dominate India?
6. What did the Aryans lay the foundations for?
7. What was the name the British gave India?
8. Name two Indian festivals from different religions.

Level 2

9. Why do you think different parts of India experience different weather patterns?
10. How do you think the Himalayas earned its name?
11. Is India a mix of nationalities? Why?
12. What does "the jewel in the crown" refer to and why do you think it was so called?
13. Why is 1947 an important year for Indians? Give two reasons.

 ISBN-978-81-8477-730-7

Level 3

14. Discuss with a partner what you think are the factors that unite India. Do the following exercises.
    - Identify the points in the given passage and list them in the form of a table like the one below.
    - Explain in what way you think the points you have listed unite people. A suggestion has been given, but you do not need to include it.

India, a community	
What unites India	**Why**
Independence Day	

Vocabulary

You have learnt earlier that the word **or** can be used as a **coordinating conjunction.**

A. The coordinating conjunction "or" is used in the first paragraph of "India, a Community". Find the sentence and write it down.

Note that the sentence you have written is a positive one. However, "or" can be used, instead of "and", in a negative sentence. Note the following example.

negative

You **can't** have rice **or** chapattis.

We can use **not only... but also** as a way of giving emphasis to additional information.

 ISBN-978-81-8477-730-7

B. Find an example in the passage *India, a Community* in which the words "not only... but also" are used.

C. Rewrite or develop the following sentences using the coordinating conjunctions "or" or "not only ... but also".

1. My favourite food is Rogan Josh.
2. You can have rice and chapatti.
3. I can't eat chicken.
4. Not only is she an excellent cook...
5. Hurry up and grate the carrots...
6. ... but also has cashew nuts.

D. Complete these sentences using "or".

1. He can't have ...
2. I don't like ...
3. They won't have ...
4. We shouldn't go ...
5. We wouldn't dare ...
6. We mustn't expect ...
7. You couldn't be ...
8. It might not ...

 ISBN-978-81-8477-730-7

E. Complete these sentences using "or else". Read them all first.

1. We'll go to Sri Lanka ...
2. We'll take the train ...
3. Then we'll go by plane ...
4. Tomorrow we'll buy the ...
5. I'll send an email ...

F. Combine these pairs of sentences using "not only... but also". You may need to reorder and drop words.

1. They are definitely the right size. They are the right colour.
2. The new road was as straight as an arrow. It was free of bumps.
3. He could find the old documents. He could tell you about their origins.
4. The lion was a handsome beast. It was free to roam the grasslands.
5. The race was utterly compelling. It was held at the new sports ground.

Grammar . Punctuation

The **apostrophe** is used to show that letters have been left out of a word. Note the following examples.

there**'**s – there **i**s

let**'**s – let **us**

 ISBN-978-81-8477-730-7

A. Look at the table below. The words in the left-hand column are all contractions, but the apostrophes are missing. Rewrite them in the next column with the apostrophe correctly placed. The first one has been done for you.

Words without apostrophes	Words with apostrophe
wont	won't
couldnt	
youre	
Id	
wouldve	

B. Using the apostrophe, shorten some of the words in the following conversation. (You will find that in doing so, it sounds more natural.)

Pradeep: I will never get this homework done. I have not got much time!

Amal: What is the homework about?

 ISBN-978-81-8477-730-7

Pradeep:	It is about the main rivers and tributaries that run through India.
Amal:	Do you not have to get it done for tomorrow?
Pradeep:	Yes, and I suppose it will take about thirty minutes to do it thoroughly.
Amal:	You will find my atlas useful then.
Pradeep:	Thanks! I am really grateful.

C. Write down the full version or shorter version of these words and expressions using the apostrophe. Time yourself!

1. will not
2. we're
3. he is
4. she is
5. that's
6. let's
7. who's
8. should not
9. there's
10. I have
11. you're
12. wouldn't
13. has not
14. could not
15. they've
16. you've

D. Correct this paragraph.

"Theyve organised a special party for the twins," said Mrs Lee to her two children, "and youre invited, so youd better be on your best behaviour."

"But were tired of visiting the twins! It wont be our idea of a party," the two children moaned.

Mrs Lee ignored their complaints. "Since theres likely to be cousins, grandparents, aunties and uncles and goodness knows who else, youll have to wear your best clothes – and dont get them dirty."

 ISBN-978-81-8477-730-7

E. Do you think the following should have an apostrophe? Add an apostrophe where you think it should go.

1. Mr and Mrs Bhatts
2. three oclock
3. Ps and Qs
4. Mrs MacDonald
5. Mrs OBrien
6. sixes and sevens
7. so on and so on
8. Dos and Donts
9. 1980s
10. BBC
11. months of the year
12. the three Rs

Listening

Listen to the piece of information and answer the questions.

1. Where is the source of the Ganges?
2. What is the length of the Ganges?
3. Where is the mouth of the Ganges?
4. Name a famous holy city by the Ganges.

 ISBN-978-81-8477-730-7

Speaking

Present a short talk to a group about the river Ganges, using information from what you heard in "Listening". Follow the guidelines below.

1. Find out the names of some of the tributaries of the Ganges and mention them in your talk.
2. Try not to read from your write-up or to use it as a prompt. Memorise what you consider to be the main points in your presentation.

Speaking Tip

It is better to know a few points well than a lot poorly.

Writing

Create a leaflet on the national symbols of India. Follow the steps below.

1. Scan the excerpt for information on symbols and find out more about each one.
2. Find examples of other symbols (such as religious symbols or symbols for birds, trees, flowers and fruit). Explain what they mean.

 ISBN-978-81-8477-730-7

3. Arrange the information in the table below.

Symbol	Category (e.g. animal)	What it means

Activity

Complete the map of India.

1. Place each symbol on the correct location on the blank map of India. You will need to refer to an atlas to make sure you have got the locations right. The rivers have been drawn for your convenience.

   - Indian Ocean – **A**
   - Bay of Bengal – **B**

 ISBN-978-81-8477-730-7

- Arabian Sea – **C**
- Thar Desert – **D**
- River Ganges – **E**
- River Godavari – **F**
- Mumbai – **G**
- Chennai – **H**
- Kolkata – **I**
- Delhi – **J**

2. Now create a key to go with the map. An example is given below.

Key

- *City*

10 Living and Working in Bangladesh

Read the following excerpt on Bangladesh from *Rivers* by Catherine Chambers.

1 The people living on a **delta** always have to be prepared for flooding. They build their homes on banks or platforms of earth. The houses are mostly made of wood and are set on stilts. Even so, flooding often causes a lot of deaths and damage to farmland.

2 In the dry winters the ground is full of large holes. This is where the earth was dug up to make the banks and platforms. The holes are called borrow pits. Water fills the pits and is used for drinking and washing. It is also used for irrigating crops.

3 Most people in Bangladesh are farmers. Two or three crops of rice are grown every year in the rich, damp soil. Tropical fruits, beans, oilseeds, wheat, vegetables, bamboo and jute are grown on the rest. Nearly a million tonnes of fish are caught every year. Most are fresh-water fish.

---

delta: a landform at the mouth of a river created by the gradual accumulation of silt

 ISBN-978-81-8477-730-7

Reading Comprehension

Answer the following questions.

Level 1

1. What do the people of Bangladesh always have to be prepared for?
2. What are the houses in Bangladesh made of?
3. What are the holes that are left when the earth is dug up called?
4. What crops are grown in Bangladesh?
5. How much fish is caught in a year in Bangladesh?

Fishing contraption, Bangladesh

Level 2

6. Why are houses built on stilts useful to the people of Bangladesh?
7. In what way do the people of Bangladesh use the soil to their benefit?
8. Can you guess why the soil is rich in Bangladesh?
9. Can Bangladesh be said to be a rich country although many of its people are poor?
10. What do you think the life of a Bangladeshi farmer must be like?

 ISBN-978-81-8477-730-7

Read the note on "topic sentence" and answer the questions that follow.

A topic sentence indicates what a passage is about and helps the reader locate the main idea. It is usually the opening sentence of a paragraph – though it may appear much later in a paragraph or even at the end.

Look at the paragraph below. The sentence in bold print is the topic sentence.

> **One of nature's greatest destroyers is flooding**. It may not seem to you as dramatic as a tornado or a hurricane, but its consequences can be just as great.

A writer will often expand on the main idea to emphasise a point, but we can look for key words that add detail to or support the main idea. The words in bold print below are key words.

> In some parts of the world such as the **Maldives** in the Indian Ocean, severe **flooding** is a real **hazard**.

Level 3

11. Study the excerpt *Living and Working in Bangladesh* and complete the table below by filling in the correct information in the space provided.

Topic	Living and Working in Bangladesh
The general subject matter of the excerpt	
The main idea in each paragraph	
The supporting details in each paragraph	

 ISBN-978-81-8477-730-7

12. Study the map. The area shaded in purple indicates places facing regular floods. What does it tell you about flooding in Bangladesh? Does it indicate the extent and degree of flooding in different areas?

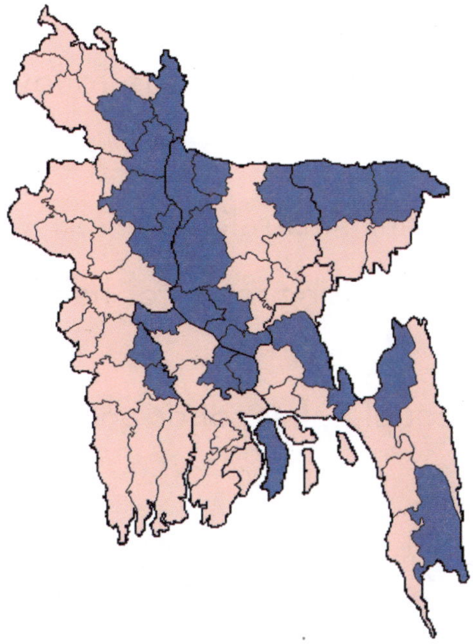

Vocabulary

Remember what an **adverb of frequency** is? It tells you **how often** something happens. Note the following examples.

Sometimes Neha takes a walk in the nearby park.

I **often** meet my teacher on the road.

A. Underline the adverbs of frequency in the following passages from *Living and Working in Bangladesh.*

1. The people living on a delta always have to be prepared for flooding. They build their homes on banks or platforms of earth. The houses are mostly made of wood and are set on stilts. Even so, flooding often causes a lot of deaths and damage to farmland.
2. Most people in Bangladesh are farmers. Two or three crops of rice are grown every year in the rich, damp soil. Tropical fruits, beans, oilseeds, wheat, vegetables, bamboo and jute are grown on the rest. Nearly a million tonnes of fish are caught every year. Most are fresh-water fish.

 ISBN-978-81-8477-730-7

Adverbs of duration indicate **how long** something takes or lasts. Note the following example.

The flood lasted for **two weeks.**

B. Identify the adverbs of duration in the following sentences and underline them.

1. They spent a week touring Australia.
2. I had been sitting in the waiting room for half an hour when Jamila appeared.
3. I went out for only a couple of seconds and when I got back the play was over.
4. We are seldom in touch these days and I haven't called her for six months.

C. Now write a sentence with each of the following adverbs of duration.

1. ... for three days and three nights
2. ... an extremely long time
3. ... hardly any time at all
4. ... a few minutes

D. Look at the adverbs in the box and do as follows.

1. Circle the adverbs of frequency.

occasionally	delicately	speedily	seldom
foolishly	frequently	generally	lazily
carefully	sometimes	always	usually

2. Think of three adverbs of frequency not already listed above and use them to make your own sentences.

 ISBN-978-81-8477-730-7

E. Underline the adverbs of duration.

1. The wind howled round the barn and through the orchard for ages.
2. Can you wait for the time being while I make the call?
3. It will take a long time to reorganise the system.
4. He waited for a second and then rushed off, I'm afraid.

F. Complete these sentences by adding such adverbs of duration as are not used in question E.

1. ______________ he'll come over to see you and answer your questions.
2. He sailed round the world ______________.
3. The fever was so bad she sat by the child's bed ______________.
4. ______________ the teacher explained how to do the complex dance movements.

Grammar

In a sentence, the subject may be directly said to be carrying out the action denoted by the verb. In such a case, the verb is considered to be in the **active voice**.

active verb

The water **soaked** the fields.

The same sentence may however be rephrased in such a way that the action seems more important than the subject. In such a case, the verb is said to be in the **passive voice**.

passive verb

The fields **were soaked** by the water.

Prepositions such as "by", "in" or "with" are used in a sentence to indicate how, where and when the action (denoted by the verb) takes place.

 ISBN-978-81-8477-730-7

A. Turn the following passive sentences into active ones. For some sentences you may have to say who or what creates the action.

1. The earth was dug up to make the banks and platforms.
2. Water is used for irrigating crops.
3. Two or three crops of rice are grown by the farmers.
4. Nearly a million tonnes of fish are caught.
5. Rice is the main crop grown by farmers.
6. Houses in Bangladesh are built on stilts.

B. Now turn the following active sentences into passive ones.

1. Water fills the pits.
2. The people work on the land.
3. They dug the soil to make the stilts for their houses.
4. The farmers grow tropical fruits, beans, oilseeds and other crops.
5. The people of Bangladesh love to eat fish.
6. Frequent floods make life difficult.

C. Which sentence is active? Which sentence is passive? Write **A** (for active) or **P** (for passive) in the brackets.

1. Joy finished her breakfast before her brother. (   )
2. The bus was stuck in the ditch. (   )
3. The dog licked Bimal's hand and face. (   )
4. The neighbour's pet rabbit was retrieved by Chen and his little sister. (   )
5. The village was covered in snow and ice. (   )

 ISBN-978-81-8477-730-7

6. The broken chair was taken away by the school keeper. ( )

7. He recognised the stolen bike immediately. ( )

8. The secret code was written in green ink. ( )

D. Change these passive sentences into active ones.

1. A page of homework was done by all the students.
2. The houses and flats were built by local builders.
3. Bread, cakes and desserts are made by the cook.
4. The tree was enveloped with blue and red lights.

E. Change these active sentences into passive ones.

1. Paul counted the pineapples.
2. The gardener cleared the leaves from the path.
3. The people fed the deer.
4. Mist surrounds the mountains.

Listening

Listen to the text and answer the questions.

1. Name some of the crafts of Bangladesh.
2. What spices are used in the cuisine?
3. What is *ilish*?
4. How is *ilish* cooked?

 ISBN-978-81-8477-730-7

Speaking

Present a short talk to a group about the cuisine of Bangladesh. Follow the given guidelines.

1. Use the information you gathered while listening to the text of "Listening".
2. Add any other information that you know about the cuisine.

Writing

Make a group of three or four and write a play together. Follow the steps below.

1. Imagine you are living in a small village community in Bangladesh when suddenly flooding takes place. Compose a short play on how you would help your family, your neighbour who happens to be an elderly man, and his dog get away.
2. If necessary, carry out some research about communities in Bangladesh and flooding. Use the library or the Internet with your teacher's guidance.
3. Take a role each and rehearse your play.
4. When you are happy with your performance, present it to another group and also watch them perform their own.

Activity

A. Collect information on the following topics and design your own fact file about Bangladesh.

1. Climate
2. Geography (landscape, terrain)
3. Rivers

 ISBN-978-81-8477-730-7

4. Seas and oceans
5. Resources (such as minerals)
6. How the land is used
7. Population
8. Location (mention the countries that border Bangladesh)

B. What else can you include in your fact file?

Dhaka port, Bangladesh

Theme 6

Animals

A. Look at the picture.

1. Who are these people?
2. What are they doing?
3. What do you think the dog is receiving?

B. Answer the following questions.

1. Do you think an animal understands what an award is?
2. Why do you think some animals seem willing to put their own lives in danger for the sake of human beings?
3. Do you think an animal can be loyal?

 ISBN-978-81-8477-730-7

11 Trixy the Wonderdog

Read the following story.

Why is Amir having a bad day? Mention the reasons.

1 Amir De Witt was having a bad day.

2 Actually, since he and his family had moved to Delhi a month ago, every day was a Bad Day. He missed everything about his old home in **Johannesburg**. He missed the view from his bedroom window; the monkey puzzle tree in their front garden; his friends; his old school; but most of all he missed Trixy, his dog.

3 "I know it's hard, darling," his mother had said, putting an arm around his shoulder, "but they won't let us take the dog to India. But Trixy will be happy here. She's going to stay with Aunty Mira and Uncle Jack. She'll be fine."

4 It was all very well, and he was sure in his heart of hearts that she *would* be fine. Uncle Jack and Aunty Mira were great, and they had a lovely farm with grounds where she could romp about to her heart's content – but what about him?

5 He missed the snuffle of her wet nose on weekday mornings, getting him up and out of bed. He missed the swish-swash of her feathery tail on his legs, the little pink pads of her paws when she jumped up to greet him, the sloppy wetness of her tongue licking his face when he came home from school each day. These days, Amir thought, he felt like One Big Missing Machine.

What are Aruna and Mona like?

6 "Hey, Witless," called out Aruna, the big bossy girl from Class VII.

7 "Yeah, Dim-witty, come over here," joined in her friend Mona.

Johannesburg: the largest city in South Africa

 ISBN-978-81-8477-730-7

8 They both collapsed laughing, like this was the biggest joke in the whole world. Amir sighed. No one in South Africa had made fun of his name. In fact, it was a pretty common name.

9 During the first period – maths – Amir sat by the window, doodling in his notebook. Instead of working, he gazed out on to the dusty playing field, and imagined Trixy dashing around outside.

10 "A-*meer*!" Mr Venkatesh suddenly shouted.

11 Amir jerked out of his daydream. "Y-yes, sir?"

12 "Would you like to share with the class what is *so* very fascinating outside?"

13 "Er... er... nothing, sir."

14 "Exactly. And nothing is what you're going to get in the next test if you don't get on with your work. Right *now*."

15 Amir turned back to his book. He found that in the margins he'd sketched a long fluffy ear, a black triangle for a nose and whiskers, four ovals and a blob that looked just like a dog's pawprint.

16 "We'll see you at breaktime, Witless," hissed Aruna from the desk behind. "And you better bring our money."

17 Oh help, thought Amir to himself. Yesterday, he'd managed to wheedle twenty rupees from his mother on the pretext that he needed a new notebook. A few days before that another fifty, saying that their class was going on a school trip. But it wasn't going to be long before his mother cottoned on to the fact that the money wasn't going anywhere but into the pockets of Awful Aruna.

18 *Trixy, Mixie, Wonderdog. Where are you?* He sent a silent plea up into the air.

 ISBN-978-81-8477-730-7

19 The words floated out of the open window and up into the air. Up, like a kite – magic words, floating out of the school yard, over the town, up and up into the clouds; above the clouds; up and away to the furthest reaches of the great velvet dark-and-light spangled sky, until...

20 ... A light flashed on the console of a strange-looking spacecraft, and a beeper went off.

21 The captain adjusted the headphones beneath his long fluffy ears. "Red alert!" he woofed into his mouthpiece. "Star Command to Trixy. Come in, Trix."

22 There was a crackle of electricity and then the captain heard a tinny voice: "Trixy to Star Command. What's the problem?"

23 "It's young Amir," the captian growled. "He's sending distress signals. You better get on it right away."

24 "On my way, sir."

25 "That dog's gone crazy," said Uncle Jack, watching Trixy spinning around. "Hey, girl, you want to go walkies?"

26 Trixy barked twice, and dashed to the back door. The moment Uncle Jack opened it, she was off like a flash of brown lightning. She rounded the corner of the yard, and screeched to a halt behind the coal shed. She concentrated with all her canine might on the little boy that she'd loved and looked after, until she could see his face clearly – the mole

 ISBN-978-81-8477-730-7

just above his right eyebrow, the shock of floppy hair, the dimple on his left cheek that appeared whenever he smiled – and the tag of her collar glowed red... redder... superbright... *Pchang*!

27 With a single great bound, she leapt into the air, paws outstretched. Trixy streaked across the sky, speeding onwards towards India.

28 The clock's hand was creeping towards eleven. Amir's hand kept creeping towards his pocket, hoping madly that by some miracle, a twenty-rupee note lay there. He was doomed.

29 How would he explain another torn shirt, and a fresh set of bruises to his mother?

30 The bell went for breaktime. Twenty-nine chairs scraped backwards, twenty-nine notebooks were flung into twenty-nine bags, and fifty-eight feet were pounding out of the door. The thirtieth pair of feet belonged to Amir De Witt, and they seemed to be glued to the floor.

31 There was no escape. Amir told his feet sternly not to be so pathetic. They moved reluctantly, first one, then the other, then the first again, until they carried him into the playground.

32 "Where's our money?" demanded Aruna, pushing her face close to his.

33 "Yeah, come on, dweeb. Cough up." Mona flicked her long pony-tail in his face and mimicked Aruna's scowl. "We know your folks are loaded, Mr Richy-rich Ambassador's son. So why not spread a little of your wealth around?"

34 "I thought I had some here," Amir stuttered, frantically searching his trouser pockets. "Maybe it fell out... erhm..."

35 "Fell out?" mocked Aruna. "If you've got so much to lose, you can just pay up *double* tomorrow."

36 "I sh-sh-shan't!" he said, desperately.

37 "Oh yeah?" The two girls advanced on him. "Well, in that case..."

38 Amir edged backwards. He winced, and closed his eyes waiting for the first punch, when suddenly – suddenly, he heard a whoosh! And a woof! And a swish-swash-swish of a feathery tail.

 ISBN-978-81-8477-730-7

39 He opened his eyes and to his amazement he saw Mona lying backwards in the dust with her legs in the air being licked to death by...

40 "*Trixy*?" Amir cried.

41 "Woof! Woof!" replied Trixy, and then bounded after Aruna, catching her skirt in her teeth.

42 Aruna fled across the yard, yelling. Trixy bounded after her, barking, her tail rotating like a helicopter, her ears flying. Aruna scooted up the nearest tree and perched in one of the lower branches, terrified.

43 Trixy bared her teeth in a pretty convincing snarl. Turning around, she trotted happily back to Amir.

44 Amir was still leaning back on the wall, stunned by the turn of events. Trixy bounded up to him and jumped up. Her paws made two dusty prints on either shoulder of his shirt, and licked his face until he thought she might lick it clean off.

45 "Trixy, you came!"

46 "Grrrruff!" she replied, which meant, in dog language, "You betcha".

47 Then she trotted a few paces ahead and stood stock still. The little red tag on her collar glowed.

48 "Trixy to Star Command. Come in, Star Command."

49 "Reading you loud and clear. What news?"

 ISBN-978-81-8477-730-7

50 "Situation sorted," she barked. Then wuffled a bit to clear her throat.

51 "Excellent work, Trixy," came the reply. "Was there something else?"

52 "Requesting permission to relocate, sir."

53 "Relocate?" barked the Captain. "What on earth are you barking about?"

54 "Well, sir," Trixy replied, "Delhi's really quite nice at this time of year, and I... well, I think the city needs me."

India Gate, Delhi

55 "Oh," wuffed the Captain sarcastically. "It does, doesn't it?"

56 "Well, sir, one corner of it, anyway," Trixy looked back at Amir.

57 There was a pause. Then the Captain's voice came through loud and clear.

58 "Permission granted," he barked. And then added in a softer voice, "Now, go walkies."

59 As he ran back home with Trixy frisking along by his side, Amir decided that Delhi looked like a pretty nice place to live in after all.

 ISBN-978-81-8477-730-7

Reading Comprehension

Answer the following questions.

Level 1

1. Where had Amir de Witt moved to and from which place?
2. Apart from Trixy, his dog, what else did Amir miss?
3. What was likely to happen to Trixy when Amir moved to India?
4. How would you sum up what Amir felt without Trixy?
5. Who teased Amir about his name?
6. What was the name of Amir's maths teacher?

Level 2

7. Who do you think is the main character of the story? Describe some of the person's physical and mental attributes using the diagram below.

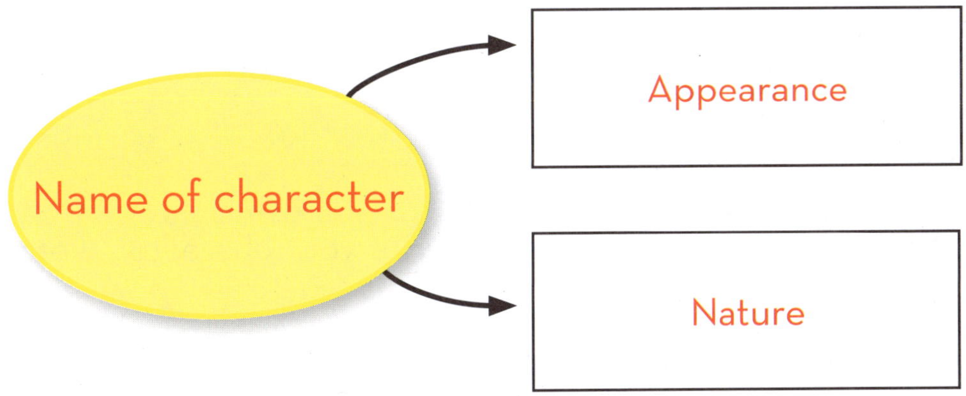

8. Do you think there is a magical element in the story? Explain your answer.
9. How does Trixy regard Amir?
10. What kind of a teacher do you think Mr Venkatesh is?
11. Why was Amir worried when Aruna asked him to bring money?
12. What is Amir's silent prayer compared to? Why?
13. Why were Amir's feet glued to the floor when the bell went for breaktime?

 ISBN-978-81-8477-730-7

14. Describe Mona's encounter with Trixy.

15. How do you think Aruna and Mona felt at the end of the story?

Level 3

16. Write two short character sketches of Aruna and Mona. Follow the steps below.

    - Complete the table below by answering the questions.

Question	Aruna	Mona
Who is she?		
What does she say about Amir?		
What does she do? (give a specific example)		
What does Amir say about her?		
What is her relationship like with the other bully?		

    - Use the information you have to write your character sketches.

Vocabulary

The word "said" is commonly used in writing speech, but it might sound repetitive if overused. The best way to avoid **overused words** would be to find other words to replace them.

In the following example, "said" is replaced by "announced" since it suits the way Trixy is talking. It also suggests that she has just arrived to offer help.

"I'm here to help!" **said** Trixy the Wonderdog.

"I'm here to help!" **announced** Trixy the Wonderdog.

 ISBN-978-81-8477-730-7

A. Scan the excerpt to find four examples of verbs that are used in speech instead of "said". Discuss with a partner why they are used.

B. Replace "said" with a suitable verb in the following sentences.

1. "Get out of my way – now!" said Aruna.
2. "Why are you staring out of the window?" said Mr Venkatesh.
3. Amir sat down with his head in his hands. "What am I to do without Trixy?" he said.
4. "I'm so pleased to see you, Trixy," said Amir.
5. "How on earth did Trixy get here?" said Amir's mother.

C. Write three less common words or phrases for each of these overused ones.

1. gave
2. lovely
3. saw
4. then

D. Our choice of words depends on what we are writing about. Read the sentences below. What is wrong with each one? Underline the unsuitable word and rewrite the sentence replacing it with a suitable one.

1. She thought that her hair was too brief, so she decided to grow it longer.
2. The dessert winds were blowing so hard that no one could travel.
3. Tommy is a very well soccer player and uses excellent tactics on the field.
4. "We all want a bit of peas and quiet!" screeched my sister from her room!

 ISBN-978-81-8477-730-7

Grammar . Punctuation

The **dash** can be used in different ways to create different effects in writing. Sometimes it is used to indicate a pause. A writer might use a dash to **add extra information** to a sentence. The dash can also be used to **give emphasis.**

Read the following example:

> "During the first period - maths - Amir sat by the window..."

Here "maths" is added to give further information regarding the "first period".

Now look at this other example:

> "Uncle Jack and Aunty Mira were great, and they had a lovely farm with ground where she [Trixy] could romp about to her heart's content - but what about him [Amir]?"

Here, the dash emphasises how Amir feels without his dog.

A. Write three sentences using the dash to add extra information. They can be about Amir, Trixy or any other character in the story.

B. Write a short paragraph and include in it a dash for emphasis. Choose your topic from one of the following situations:

1. Trixy meets Amir's mother again.
2. Mr Venkatesh is very pleased with Amir's work.
3. Aruna and Mona are transformed into helpful and happy girls.

 ISBN-978-81-8477-730-7

An **ellipsis** (usually three dots) is used to show that some things have been deliberately left unsaid. It usually occurs when:

- someone is interrupted during a dialogue.
- a speech tails off unfinished.
- someone is lost for words.

C. In what way is the ellipsis used in the following example from the story?

"Er... er... nothing, sir."

D. Write a short dialogue between Amir and Mr Venkatesh, using the ellipses at a point where Mr Venkatesh interrupts Amir.

Listening

Can you make out the feelings expressed in the passage from the story? How is each of the characters feeling and why? Note that they may be experiencing more than one kind of emotion. Describe their feelings by completing the table below.

Feelings		
Trixy	**Amir**	**Aruna**

 ISBN-978-81-8477-730-7

Speaking

Work in pairs. Take turns with a partner to explain what happens in the story. Make your presentation as entertaining as possible. Keep the following guidelines in mind.

1. Rely on what you remember of the story.
2. You can narrate one half and your partner can narrate the other.
3. You can decide between the two of you who would begin.

Writing

Write a story about a remarkable animal. Follow the steps below and fill up the chart for your convenience:

1. Choose an animal. It could be a common or unique pet.
2. Think about the sequence of events in your story and complete the table.

   You can always change your story as you write.
3. Introduce some magic into your story. Use *Trixy the Wonderdog* as a model, but the idea should be your own.
4. If you want, you can use the first-person narrative and write the story in an autobiographical style.

 ISBN-978-81-8477-730-7

5. Decide on a suitable title for your story once you have completed it.

Ideas for my story	
Characters (heroes and villains)	
Setting for the story (city or countryside - or any other location)	
What happens (the conflict, obstacle or problem that drives your story)	
Ending (think of a possible resolution of the conflict)	

Activity

Write a leaflet about what you think would be the best way to tackle bullying. Follow the guidelines below.

1. Chalk out your points before you begin.
2. Your advice could include the following suggestions.
    - Seeking help and not suffering in silence
    - Finding trusted adults, such as parents, carers or teachers, whom you can confide in
    - Writing down your concerns
    - Keeping a record of each experience of bullying

 ISBN-978-81-8477-730-7

3. Make a checklist of the typical features of bullying. The following are a few examples.
    - Threatening behaviour
    - Hitting or other forms of physical contact
    - Forcing you to hand over money
    - Cyber bullying (over the Internet or a mobile phone)
4. When you feel you have enough information, design your leaflet.

 ISBN-978-81-8477-730-7

12 Mirror Work

Read the following account of an investigation into animal intelligence, written by Mary Green.

1 There are several studies that attempt to test an animal's intelligence. One of the most well-tried is the self-recognition test, usually called the mirror self-recognition test. Marks are placed on the animal's body and the animal can only see them if a mirror is used. Researchers observe whether or not the animal takes any notice of the marks. This experiment is based on the idea that if an animal can recognise itself then it must have some degree of intelligence, because it shows an awareness of itself – something that humans have.

2 You could say, of course, that it is simple coincidence or that some other sense is being used when the animal appeared to be curious about the marks on its body. So the test is carried out many times, and if the animal examines the marks again and again, it is likely to be intelligent behaviour.

? What is the topic sentence of paragraph 2?

3 You could also argue that another sense is being used and this encourages the animal to examine the marks and that it is not evidence of self-awareness. Consequently, researchers carrying out the test also apply invisible marks and observe the animal's behaviour.

? What is the topic sentence of paragraph 3?

 ISBN-978-81-8477-730-7

4 Chimpanzees seem to perform well on the mirror test, but not necessarily other **primates**. Dolphins seem to be interested in marks on their bodies too. Several tests have been carried out on dolphins and in particular it was found that some dolphins used the mirror and other "reflective surfaces" to study their marks more often than when they had no marks. It must be difficult to test a dolphin in water! So scientists may find other ways of conducting such tests. We may find out in the future.

Reading Comprehension

Answer the following questions.

Level 1

1. What is the test mentioned in the above passage that aims to assess an animal's intelligence?
2. What equipment and process was used in the test?
3. What were the researchers involved in the test observing?
4. Which animals do not necessarily perform well in the test?

---

primates: animals such as monkeys and apes, which belong to the mammal order named "primates" and are distinguished by large brains, hands and feet. Human beings are also considered part of this order.

 ISBN-978-81-8477-730-7

5. How do dolphins respond to the test?

6. Why is it difficult to test dolphins?

Level 2

7. Why is the particular intelligence test mentioned in the account chosen?

8. How do human beings express self-awareness?

9. The passage mentions two possible arguments against the test. What is the first one?

10. Mention the second argument.

11. How does the test counter the two arguments?

Read the following note on supporting evidence and answer the questions.

In the above passage the scientific statements are accompanied by **supporting evidence**. Just like supporting details, it gives extra information about a topic. However, supporting evidence gives the **reasons for** or **consequences of** a phenomenon. It might also **illustrate** or **emphasise** something to back the main statements.

Level 3

12. The following connectors provide a cue or signpost for the supporting evidence in *Mirror Work*. Locate the connectors and the supporting evidence they introduce in the paragraphs and complete a table like the one below.

Paragraph	Connector	Supporting evidence
1	because	
2	So	
3	Consequently	
4	in particular	

 ISBN-978-81-8477-730-7

Vocabulary

Look at Unit 8 once more and review the concept of connectors of cause and effect. Note that they link ideas together and help to make what you read and write coherent.

Below are some other types of **connectors that are meant to support evidence**.

Connectors that illustrate

as shown by	as revealed by	in the case of
such as	for instance	for example

Connectors that emphasise

above all else | especially | particularly | significantly

A. Underline the connectors in the following paragraph and jot down their type.

Dolphins were chosen for study since the researchers wanted to find out if they showed intelligent behaviour. The dolphins showed a genuine interest in the marks placed on their bodies. For instance, they examined them in mirrors and other "reflective surfaces". Significantly, chimps seem very good at taking tests of intelligence. Elephants are also capable of undertaking the mirror test. As a result of such experiments, scientists feel encouraged to investigate animal intelligence further. Consequently further tests are likely to be carried out.

 ISBN-978-81-8477-730-7

B. Make sentences with the following connectors. Indicate the type of connector within brackets next to the sentence.

1. Moreover
2. Noticeably
3. For instance
4. As can be seen/witnessed

C. Quickly write down in the box three connectors that illustrate.

Connectors that illustrate:

D. Rewrite these sentences by adding connectors that illustrate. Use a different connector for each sentence.

1. Some rhinos – the black rhino – are endangered species.
2. All his books do well and his second book, which came out last year, was a best seller.
3. Discovered treasure is often worth little, but the Bactrian treasure hoard in Afghanistan is invaluable.

E. Quickly write down in the box three connectors that emphasise.

Connectors that emphasise:

 ISBN-978-81-8477-730-7

F. Rewrite these sentences by adding connectors that emphasise. Use a different connector for each sentence.

1. The scarves produced by the weavers had brilliant patterns and colours.
2. She is accomplished at playing the guitar, the harp and the violin, but it is the sitar that is her real forte.
3. I love curries of all kinds but vegetable vindaloo is my favourite.

Grammar

Quantifying determiners tell us roughly how many or how much of a certain thing is being spoken about in a sentence.

For example:

> There were **a few** dolphins in the water and **some** people were watching them.

Certain quantifiers, such as "much" and "many", may be used in the wrong way. Make sure you use "many" and "a few" with nouns that you can count (countable nouns) and "much" and "less" with nouns that you can't count (uncountable nouns). A few examples are given below:

many pens   a few pens   much food   less food

A. Can you spot a quantifying determiner in the following sentences from *Mirror Work*? If you can, underline them.

1. There are several studies that attempt to test an animal's intelligence.
2. So the test is carried out many times, and if the animal examines the marks again and again, it is likely to be intelligent behaviour.
3. Some dolphins used the mirror and other "reflective surfaces" to study their marks more often than when they had no marks.

 ISBN-978-81-8477-730-7

B. Write a sentence with each of the following quantifiers (remember that some quantifiers can be used with both countable and uncountable nouns):

1. many
2. a few
3. much
4. less
5. several
6. some

C. Circle the quantifying determiners in the box.

many	street	feet	expect	people	remember	vehicle	few
the	her	flower	orchid	plenty	much	pencil	some
noun	verb	work	reach	several	coach	them	it
speak	less	we	teach	special			

D. Choose the most suitable word from the given options to add to these sentences. Write it in the correct place and change the punctuation if necessary.

1. There's space to park the car if you're careful.

   a. another   b. enough   c. any

2. Have you taken the tomatoes from the fridge?

   a. all   b. a little   c. every

3. Time was wasted waiting for the bus to arrive.

   a. both   b. each   c. a lot of

 ISBN-978-81-8477-730-7

4. Is there ink left in the printer?

a. any b. the other c. either

5. The children have a packed lunch to take on the trip.

a. neither b. less c. each

6. The train is due in twenty minutes.

a. no b. the other c. another

Listening

Listen to the text and answer the following questions.

1. How are dolphins usually depicted with humans in ancient art?
2. Who was Arion?
3. Where was Taras located? Where is it now?
4. When was *Boy on a Dolphin* made?
5. How was the dolphin depicted in the movie?

Speaking

Present a short talk about *Boy on a Dolphin*.

1. Draw on the information in the "Listening" section.
2. Include any further information you know about dolphins.

 ISBN-978-81-8477-730-7

Writing

Write an account about the high intelligence of chimpanzees taking the following points into account.

1. Chimpanzees are closely related to humans.
2. They have strong relationships and live in large groups.
3. They use simple tools (such as stones to crack nuts).
4. They make simple weapons (such as spears from sticks) to hunt small animals.
5. A chimpanzee performs well on the mirror test, showing an awareness of itself (as a dolphin does).

Remember

- You must establish the main points you make, so you must give supporting evidence.
- Use appropriate connectors to present the supporting evidence.
- Review the work you have done in this unit to help you.

 ISBN-978-81-8477-730-7

Activity

Find out what other animals have the capability to pass the mirror test and create a poster on them. A few suggestions are given below.

1. Choose one or two animals.
2. Follow the guidelines below and design a poster on intelligent animals.
   - Include a collage of the animals you mention.
   - You could use cut-outs from magazines as well as your own illustrations.
   - You may design your poster on a computer with your teacher's help.
3. Briefly describe the animals' skills. You could write in the form of headings or short sentences.
4. Include information on how we treat these animals. Take your cue from the questions below.
   - Do any of them belong to an endangered species?
   - Are any of their habitats in danger?
5. Think of a good heading for your poster.

 ISBN-978-81-8477-730-7